INTEGRITY AT WORK
IN FINANCIAL SERVICES

Securities & Investment Institute
8 Eastcheap
London EC3M 1AE

Telephone: +44 (0)20 7645 0600
Facsimile: +44 (0)20 7645 0601
Company Registration No. 2687534
Registered Charity No. 1036566

ISBN: 978-1-906917-25-8

First edition, printed May 2009

Printed and bound in Great Britain by BHF Graphics Ltd, Dartford, Kent.

CONTENTS

INTRODUCTION

Since the Securities & Investment Institute published its first book of dilemmas in June 2007, the financial world has gone through a period of unprecedented upheaval, with many of the apparent certainties of those who joined the industry over the last ten years being swept away.

However, one thing that has not changed is the need to embrace the central tenet of these books; namely, adherence to the highest standards of integrity and ethical behaviour. Indeed, public expectation now is that standards of behaviour in all spheres need to be substantially improved if the industry is to start to rebuild the trust that has been forfeited by the events of the past eighteen months.

Perhaps nowhere is this better illustrated than in the spotlight now being shone on remuneration policies where governments, regulators and professional bodies, including the Securities & Investment Institute, have responded publicly to the ethical inconsistencies in remuneration policies, which appear to reward failure as highly as success, particularly when success turns out to have been transitory, whereas the impact of failure may be long-lasting.

The standards of integrity required by the case studies in this new book arguably are higher today than when the first book was launched and to illustrate this we offer 12 new scenarios for you to consider. These have been arranged in two sections, each of which contains six dilemmas. The first section is intended to appeal to those still building their career, whilst the second should resonate with more established practitioners.

I am pleased to invite you to join the 60,000 readers of the first book in considering, in your own business environment, application of the principles contained in this new book.

Scott J Dobbie CBE, FSI(Hon) - Chairman, Securities & Investment Institute

ACKNOWLEDGEMENTS

Grateful thanks to the members of the Securities & Investment Institute's Integrity & Ethics Committee, who have contributed their years of wisdom and experience in the review of the cases in this book. Thanks also to those members of the Institute who kindly have contributed cases based upon their own professional experience.

The result is a collection of scenarios which are based upon, or in some cases are close reconstructions of, actual events. These cases formed the basis for the monthly Grey Matters series in the Securities & Investment Review.

Although in each case there is an optimum solution offered to readers, it is not claimed that there is a definitive right answer to many of the situations and there are those where readers may feel that an alternative solution to that offered would be equally acceptable.

ETHICS AND THE CITY

By David Lascelles

The City is in the doghouse; there is hardly a more polite way of putting it. With the world engulfed by the worst economic crisis in living memory, a furious public has fixed on the finance industry as the culprit. Top bankers have been hauled in front of MPs to issue apologies, flash City types are vilified in the media, hardly a day goes by without some new accusation. The charges are many: greed, recklessness, arrogance, short-termism and much more. The atmosphere is so highly charged that it is almost impossible to have a rational discussion about bankers without someone losing their temper.

The loss of public confidence in the City can seldom have been so severe, and the City faces a long uphill task in trying to restore it. But the remedial work is already starting. Talk around the City suggests a process of self-examination is at work and an acceptance that there were failures, that things must change if the City is to reinforce professional standards and protect its prospects. Some of the issues are quite technical, like the effectiveness of regulation and governance, others have to do with the attitude and behaviour of bankers where issues of ethics and responsibility come into play.

BLAME FOR THE CRISIS

How much were bankers to blame?

These have been exceptional times. Apart from a few ups and downs, the last decades saw near-perfect conditions for the financial markets: strong economies, rising profits, a boom in M&A and growing personal wealth. But there were unhealthy trends as well, notably too much easy money. This fuelled a massive lending boom in the property market, and also drove yields down to record lows, forcing the industry to find new ways to bump up returns. This meant taking on extra risk, but that seemed safe thanks to newfangled derivatives which insured against default.

A balanced view of the banks' role would have to say that they were not so much leading the party as reacting to favourable conditions that had been created by governments and central banks. But it would also have to say that they went too far. By the time the boom reached its peak in the summer of 2007, the amount of risk taken on by the banks was way over the top and ready to crash. There was also, within the banks, an apparent blindness to risk, a ravenous appetite for business and a sense of invulnerability which is easy to explain but less easy to excuse.

This is not a view that is universally held, by any means. Many people outside the City would see it as too indulgent to the banks because it ascribes to them a contributory rather than a central role. They would also say that it shifts too much of the blame on to the managers of the global economy when the banks not only piled up the fuel for the crisis but also ignited it.

History will be the judge. But today's reality is that public opinion has got the banks firmly in its sights and they will find it hard to escape. This means that public opinion will have to be mollified before the banks can recover their position, which could happen in a number of ways.

One is that the City will have to accept "punishment" in the form of tougher controls on matters like bonuses, in heavier regulation, and a barrage of criticism that may go on for some time, possibly years.

Another is that the industry will find itself "demoted" in political and social terms. Admitting to being a banker will – already does – attract wry comment. Banking may become a less desirable profession. It will be on the back foot in any debate about its future. It may even become boring.

A third is that the City will have to show a measure of contrition, which takes effort and time. When the chairmen of Royal Bank of Scotland and HBOS made their *mea culpas* in the televised Commons hearings, the public delighted at the sight, but was not convinced they were truly repentant. "Just words" was a typical comment. Contrition is not something that can be offered in a moment, like an apology; it requires a form of behaviour over the longer term. It also needs to come with a plan to put things right.

However the City does not always find it easy to admit fault. In the many conversations I have had with bankers, insurers, fund managers, brokers etc since the crisis began there has been a measure of contrition, but also an amount of defiance. "Why are they blaming us when others were at fault too?" is a typical remark. The hapless Alan Greenspan's handling of US monetary policy invariably comes up as a target. The Financial Services Authority is singled out for incompetence, No. 10 for complacency. There is also strong resentment at the political witch-hunt, which City people feel is unnecessarily adding to its reputational damage, even if it is satisfying the country's lust for blood.

Bankers may be right to expect others to share the blame. Unfortunately, episodes like Sir Fred Goodwin's pension merely confirm the public's view of the City as greedy and arrogant. The prejudice runs deep.

THE ROW OVER BONUSES

Much the most inflammatory public issue is remuneration: the sight of well-heeled bankers earning huge sums for pushing around other people's money has become abhorrent. This is overlaid by the suspicion that bonuses are not even well-earned: many are guaranteed and most are safely banked by the time the risks taken to earn them come home to roost.

That the City has been guilty of greed is, I think, beyond question, even if it is, as some people argue, a necessary part of capitalism. And many people in the City believe it will have to be curbed, as much for business as for ethical reasons: it increases risk and undermines professional standards. "There are people who don't realise how lucky they are and have some obligation back to society", says Lindsay Tomlinson, vice-chairman of Barclays Global Investors.

The bonus culture cannot be eradicated; it is a deeply rooted part of the City scene. But it will have to be made more acceptable. The question is whether this will happen through official action or City initiative. Much official action is already on the cards: the FSA will build incentive structures into banks' risk profiles, the G20 summit in London in April 2009 agreed to tackle bank remuneration, and the UK Treasury has asked Sir David Walker to come up with proposals. But it would be far better if the City managed to get on top of the problem itself. It would demonstrate a determination to deal with a crucial issue which would do much to rebuild public confidence. It would also give a stronger guarantee of success by curbing the absurd competition for talent which drives bonuses in the first place.

That is why home-grown initiatives, such as that mobilised by the Securities & Investment Institute, should be encouraged. Elements of such a plan would need to include a stronger link between performance and reward, a long-term view and a clearer alignment of employees' interests with those of other stakeholders.

Stephen Green, chairman of HSBC, says: "It should be possible to work out what is good practice, to align employees' interests with those of the owners, taking account of the longer term, the client interest and banks' position in society."

THE ROLE OF SHORT-TERMISM

Only slightly less inflammatory than pay is the issue of short-termism, another feature of the City's behaviour which the public has seized on as unacceptable. The perception that the City deals mainly for short-term gain is widely held and has been fuelled by the enormous growth of the private equity and hedge funds businesses. But more widely, there is a view that the crisis occurred because the City is simply not interested in long term results. This is not a debate about whether investors do better or worse by taking a short view, but about values which society holds dear.

The short-termist debate is not new, but it has been thrown into sharper focus by the crisis. It has also produced a new angle: the view that banks should manage their capital for the longer term, by salting more of it away in the good times so that they have something for the bad. This is not only prudent, the argument goes, but "responsible" in that it should curb excess and show that banks do not expect society to bail them out every time there is a downturn. Stephen Green, who is keen on the idea, sees this putting what he calls "a regulator" on financial activity, smoothing out the ups and downs.

That there is an ethical issue here, at least in the eyes of the broad British public, is clear. Public opinion equates short-term dealing with heartless capitalism, whereas it sees long-termism fostering stability, creating jobs, encouraging research and development.

This is a harder issue to address than remuneration because the City does not necessarily recognise a problem and, even if it does, it has difficulty coming up with clear answers. Nor can the regulator impose long-termism on the City: only the Treasury can encourage it through tax incentives and even they do not always work.

Many fund managers say that they would prefer to invest for the long term if they could. But the pressures to deliver short-term results are very powerful, particularly in bull markets. "I am not convinced you can forget the short term," says Lindsay Tomlinson of BGI. "Is it best to invest purely for the long term? Not necessarily. It might just take pressure off companies to perform."

Nonetheless, there are a number of initiatives in the City to promote long-termism, such as the aptly named Marathon Club which encourages pension funds and institutional investors to look ahead. Stephen Green of HSBC says: "The main responsibility of anyone is the maximisation of the long-term interests of the business. The 'value of values' becomes apparent when you think long term."

SELLING COMPANIES SHORT

Another "short" issue is short-selling. Again, this is standard City practice, generally tolerated, if not actually approved, by the FSA. Most people in the City would say that short-selling is not only acceptable but necessary because it keeps markets balanced by creating a "sell side" - except in a few extreme cases where speculators set out to destroy a company. But outside the City it is perceived to be cynical and anti-social. Why should hedge funds be allowed to earn billions by selling companies short? The fact that insurance companies and pension funds actually lend stock out to enable short-selling to happen is a further source of puzzlement.

As with short-termism, this contrast in views makes it difficult to sort out the rights and wrongs. The City's critics see it as unethical because it creates a misalignment between the interests of the shareholders and the company and puts businesses and jobs at risk. Insofar as the City sees it as an ethical issue, shorting is good because it leads to more efficient markets, from which everyone benefits. It can also hasten change in companies which are being badly run and are therefore, in a sense, wasteful and "anti-social".

Sir Sandy Crombie, chief executive of Standard Life, one of the UK's largest investors, believes that despite the controversy, short-selling is legitimate. "Most investors try to transact without moving the market. Some short-sellers, on the other hand, use the mechanism to move markets for their benefit. Nevertheless, short-selling helps makes markets work, so with appropriate controls in place, it should be allowed." His company lends out stock for short-selling, though it has temporarily curtailed the practice because of the risk that borrowers might not be able to give it back in current conditions.

CONFLICTS OF INTEREST

Another big question over the City's integrity has to do with conflict of interest. The perception is that integrated banks, which trade both in their own interest and that of their clients, take advantage of their two-handed position to make undeserved profits. Insider dealing is, of course, a serious offence, and banks are obliged to erect internal "Chinese Walls" to prevent it happening. But, even if banks do not intentionally breach the walls, the temptation to use unauthorised information is strong. The FSA has found evidence of unusual share price movements ahead of takeover bids in recent years.

But the issue of conflict of interest is wider than that. Banks have a fiduciary duty to put their clients' interests first and this is a key part of the City's professional code. Did they always do this in the hectic run-up to the crash? Did huge incentive payments encourage investment bankers to push through deals which were not suitable for their clients? Whose interest were they really serving at the end of the day?

This is a clear-cut issue. If a bank does a deal which it knows is not in the client's best interest, it has behaved unethically. Stephen Green is concerned by recent trends. "The City might be said to have lost its sense of suitability. It is as if people thought that so long as a transaction can be priced and is legal, it's all you need to ask. This propensity has been aggravated by the incentive structure."

One of the difficulties in caring for a client's best interests has been the decline of relationship banking. These days, banks may not even know the client for whom they are acting or, if they do, it is only on a one-off rather than an on-going basis. The "originate and distribute" model which flourished in the run-up to the crisis saw banks putting together credit deals and packaging them into securities for re-sale to other investors. This meant that the original owner of the deal shed the relationship and the new one never had it. In such conditions it is easy to ignore, even become cynical about the client.

Whether "Originate & Distribute" survives the crisis is moot. The regulator is hoping to discourage it, prudent managements increasingly see it as a source of risk as much as profit and ethically it undermines fiduciary duty. But like short-selling, it does play a role in making markets more efficient and bringing down the cost of capital, which gives it "social value". It is also doubtful whether, once such a technique has been invented, it can be stuffed back in the bottle. Securitisation may lie low for a while, but it will be back. Alan Yarrow, chairman of the London Investment Bankers Association (LIBA), says: "It wasn't all bad. We must be careful not to throw out the good with the bad."

But the concern remains. Restoring suitability as a central part of the City's ethical code will be one of the key tasks of the City's drive to re-establish its reputation and show that it has social awareness.

STRONGER GOVERNANCE

Much of what outsiders criticise about the City comes down to its behaviour: selfishness, brazenness, materialism, aggressiveness – all well caricatured by Tom Wolf's "masters of the universe". Even if such traits are not the norm, they were around enough in recent years to drive the City to excess. How is it that such behaviour can take root when it is not only offensive to others, but also puts businesses at risk?

Here we get into questions of management and governance in an intensely competitive business, where success is measured in profit and not necessarily in standards of social behaviour. Were the institutional structures inside banks strong enough to keep them in order, to ensure that the business was run prudently and ethically? Judging by recent events, the answer has to be no, though obviously there are exceptions. The task of managing today's banking giants poses a massive challenge to ordinary humans and sometimes things get out of control.

We have already seen many of the causes: bad incentive schemes, complex innovation, conflicts of interest, the decline of ethical standards and relationship banking. To these might be added what has been called the "one-way bet" mentality: the belief that governments and central banks will always bail out banks' mistakes at the end of the day. Some of it is also linked to lack of experience. Many people in the City's trading rooms, even middle management, probably never went through a serious financial crisis before this one, and lacked the necessary scars. Alan Yarrow of LIBA regrets that older people in the business had increasing difficulty being heard in the run-up to the crisis: no one believed their warnings. "Grey hair was undermined by the huge amounts of liquidity in the markets". There was also a naïve belief in the effectiveness of systems and controls, in the superiority of theory over practice. Stephen Green recalls being told by a senior fund manager that the City was enjoying "the golden age of risk management".

It is perhaps worrying that after years of Higgs-driven reforms, governance should still be perceived as weak. Among the many reasons blamed for the crisis are the failure of non-executive directors to stand up to strong executives, the inadequacy of information flows to the board, and poor understanding of the nature of the business. Whether Higgs' reforms were even effective can be questioned. It is interesting to observe that HSBC, which did not conform to Higgs, insofar as its chairman is a former chief executive, has come through the crisis in better shape than RBS, which conformed fully.

Perhaps the City could do a better job of explaining itself to the public, instead of cultivating a mystique of infallibility. The essence of capitalism is the balance between risk and reward. This means there cannot be a "bullet-proof system": there will be crises and failures at all levels: systemic, institutional, individual products, and society needs to be aware of this if it wants to enjoy the fruits of healthy markets. But at the moment, the public is not willing to heed this message, which tilts the playing field even further against the City.

THE ROLE OF SHAREHOLDERS

But if banks were failing to control their charges, were the shareholders doing any better? Hector Sants, chief executive of the FSA, has castigated "uncritical" investors for being "too reliant and unchallenging" and preferring to sell out of companies that they were worried about, rather than seeking change.

This is a criticism that is firmly rejected by the institutional investor industry. Sir Sandy Crombie at Standard Life, who previously ran the asset management side of the business, says that while shareholders can – and do – have views, they do not have levers of control. "Boards and executives need to be given – and take – responsibility for the workings of the machinery. Responsibility for the running of companies cannot be shifted to shareholders." Lindsay Tomlinson at BGI shares this view. "There is scope to disagree on where responsibility should be divided between companies and their shareholders. In theory, shareholders can do more, but it's difficult in practice. You can't easily get rid of a board if you think it's poor." However the political and the regulatory pressure is now on institutional investors to become more proactive and perform more of a watchdog role.

BACK TO SIMPLE BANKS?

If many of the failings of modern banking can be blamed on its complexity – conflicts of interest, weak governance, a loss of contact with society – the answer may lie in making it more simple. There is already much debate about the need to separate out the gung-ho investment banking side from the more staid high street side – a division which was legally enforced in the US until 1999, and existed by tradition in the City until Big Bang in 1986. The cultures and ethical viewpoints of the two are so completely different, the one "eating what it kills" and the other "eating what it grows".

Such a division would untangle conflicting interests, would enable the commercial side to build stronger client relationships and would restore public confidence in the high street. It would also simplify the social question of how to deal with banks in a crisis: the high street side would be tightly regulated and guaranteed, the investment side would be freer and capable of being cut loose if it got into trouble. Ethically, there would also be a clearer distinction between high street banks with their duty of care and investment banks with their transaction-based approach.

Stephen Green thinks we may be heading in this direction: "There will be a reversion to simplicity, at least for a while." Alan Yarrow even sees a return of the traditional "partnership culture", with its distinctive professional and business standards, in which members had a sense of ownership of the brand name. He says: "There was a natural understanding that you take money out when times are good but you put it back when times are bad. You were judged by, and you judged, like-minded people."

REFORMING CITY BEHAVIOUR

So the City has work to do to put its ethical house in order or risk a severe political and regulatory crackdown. Although steps will be needed to deal with specific issues like pay and governance, the real challenge is instilling values in the City that rebuild trust and make it more acceptable to society at large. Some of these relate to individual behaviour, some to the culture of individual institutions and many to the City's communal need to have a strong reputation for its own good.

This will not be easy, because ethical behaviour is hard to sustain in the City's competitive environment. It is easily trampled in the rush. Some people even see little value in it, particularly in today's climate when all firms, good and bad, get tarred with the same brush. It will require the City to suppress some of its competitive instincts in favour of a common approach, knowing that it is in its own interests to do so. High standards of behaviour and a responsible view of finance's social duty loom large in the public's expectations.

Sir Sandy Crombie has led major change at Standard Life that has affected employees, clients and investors alike and required the support of all of them. In seeking their backing, he tries not to lose sight of what, for them, is the key question: "Should I trust you to deliver on my behalf?"

He says: "Trust from stakeholders has to be earned. You can't demand it. In the short term, you can't do more than promise. In the long run consistent behaviour and delivery will earn you their powerful backing."

David Lascelles is Senior Fellow of the Centre for the Study of Financial Innovation and a former banking editor of the Financial Times.

case studies 1-6

perks of office

customer relations

a question of degree

recruitment commission

redundancy

wealth manager incentives

PERKS OF OFFICE

You become aware that some members of staff have been using airline promotional travel rewards, generated by travellers on company business, for personal travel, because your firm has no policy covering their use.

BACKGROUND

You are the new administration manager of a London based bank incorporated three years ago and you have responsibility for all "back office" matters.

Senior "front office" staff have been travelling extensively for the bank to promote its business and a junior member of the administration team looks after all business travel arrangements and flight booking. She has taken over only recently from a more senior administrator, who has recently left the department to join another firm.

The amount of overseas business travel is running at a high level, incurring significant expense and your MD asks you to consider ways of curtailing these costs.

One of your team mentions to you that the bank has accumulated a substantial number of air miles as it is the bank's policy to accrue air miles generated by business travel in its name, rather than permit staff to collect them personally. No attempt seems to have been made to use these air miles to defray the cost of business trips and there are no other policies or rules covering the air miles scheme, leading you to conclude that there exists some general uncertainty about these arrangements.

On investigating the air miles total, which proves to be very substantial, you notice that while no business flights have ever been booked, surprisingly, there appear to be a number of flights booked in the personal names of both the former administrator and her successor, who is now responsible for the scheme's administration.

Analysis of the records indicates that these flights were for holiday purposes, judging by the destinations, the fact that the air miles were also used for hotel bookings and that, on at least one occasion, a non-member of staff also travelled. It transpires that the non-member of staff was the former administrator's boyfriend.

You interview your junior administrator, who appears somewhat naïve and who says that her predecessor told her that the former head of administration had said that it was OK to use the air miles in this way. You also contact the former administrator who confirms what you have already heard, namely that your predecessor had said that it was acceptable for her to use the air miles as a perk. When you express surprise that her boyfriend had his travel and accommodation paid for by the bank, she replies that the bank did not pay for anything; she and her boyfriend had paid all of the airport taxes, "which were a lot of money" and they only used the air miles. She repeats that her former boss knew about this and permitted it.

Upon checking, you ascertain that there is nothing in writing to confirm what you have been told and there is absolutely nothing in the bank's procedures to cover this situation.

Accordingly, you decide to contact your predecessor, who has now retired, and ask him whether he did, in fact, give permission for these two administration staff, or indeed anyone else, to use the bank's air miles for private travel and accommodation.

He says that he really cannot remember specific situations and is generally vague about the whole matter, leaving you feeling somewhat uncomfortable about the situation with which you are now faced.

To complicate matters further, the team member who first informed you of the bank's air miles account complains to you that it is unfair that only those staff directly responsible for administering the air miles scheme can benefit from it. He considers that everyone in the back office should be able to benefit.

OPTIMUM SOLUTION

There are a number of issues which may influence how you respond to this situation:

- There are no bank procedures to control the scheme.
- Two staff who have been responsible for administering the air miles scheme have benefited personally from it.
- It is unclear whether the former head of administration actually gave permission to any of his staff to use the air miles for personal travel.
- It is unacceptable that only staff responsible for administering the scheme benefit personally from the air miles, with no specific permission being given, and with no formal scheme rules or independent controls.
- You have received a complaint from another staff member about the apparent unfairness of the distribution of bank air miles.
- The bank itself is not benefiting from its substantial air miles balance, which could be used to reduce business travel costs.
- According to your in-house legal counsel, you have no tangible evidence that the staff members concerned have actually done anything illegal.

POSSIBLE COURSES OF ACTION

- You might seek to obtain re-payment from the former administrator of the value of the flights/accommodation she and her boyfriend enjoyed.
- You could indicate to her that there will be a late P11D submission to HMRC for the value of the flights and hotel accommodation, which should have been declared as a benefit in kind.
- You may wish to reconsider the wording of the written reference that the bank gave to her present employer, which asked about honesty and integrity.

The practical difficulty with the three options above is that while you may question the honesty of the former administrator, because of your predecessor's unhelpful attitude, there is no proof of wrong-doing.

Notwithstanding these difficulties you should:

- Introduce formal written procedures for the administration of the air miles scheme and circulate them to all staff. The procedures should include a requirement to obtain appropriate senior approval for all flight/hotel bookings.
- Decide formally whether company air miles may be used only for business travel or whether a proportion may be 'given' to staff as an incentive.
- Develop and publish a demonstrably fair distribution method, applicable to all staff.
- Immediately advise your current administrator that, pending application of the new policy, any proposed use of company air miles must be signed off by you.

CONCLUSION

Although issues such as that referred to above may not, of themselves, appear significant, recent media stories demonstrate that they do have the ability to generate a lot of attention. In public bodies this is likely to engender the view that no-one in public life should receive any benefit that is not open and transparent. The question might then reasonably be asked, "Why should it be any different in business?"

The response ought to be that standards of openness and transparency should be no different in public or corporate life, even if the rewards themselves may be.

Consequently, and as suggested above, the introduction of a documented procedure, together with its formal application, is essential to prevent the continuation of this unsatisfactory and opaque situation which, if left unchecked, is likely to fester, generating ill-will and possible general disregard for rules and policies.

The response of the former administrator, suggesting that only cash counts as payment, is a mistaken view that also needs to be dispelled. There is an often expressed belief that because an item referred to does not involve actual cash, it has no value. However, the reality is that air miles have a value akin to that of the future cost of the travel to which the holder is entitled which, in a business, might be a significant amount, running into thousands of pounds.

QUICK READ SUMMARY

PERKS OF OFFICE

What is/would be unethical

To allow certain members of staff to continue to take advantage of an unofficial "perk" which can have significant monetary benefit, while not making the same opportunities available to all staff.

It would also be wrong to decide that the air miles gained through expenditure by the bank on business travel can be used by members of staff for private travel, unless this policy has been specifically sanctioned at an appropriate level.

Key points summary

Business travel by staff members has generated a significant loyalty bonus in the form of air miles from the airline used.

The bank has no policy about the use of these air miles.

Certain members of staff have used some of the air miles for personal travel.

The apparent authoriser of this use of a bank asset is unhelpful in confirming whether or not he actually authorised certain staff to use the air miles.

Adverse consequences

Failure to take any action to curb certain members of staff taking advantage of what appears to be a loophole in bank policy may encourage a generally lax culture towards compliance with policies, as well as promoting envy between staff who may benefit from this perk and those who may not.

Optimum approach

Immediately ensure that no further use of air miles is permitted until clarification is given as to the circumstances permitting their use.

Appropriate policy must be formulated regarding future use and circulated to all staff.

Policy should be regularly reviewed to ensure that it continues to be appropriate to changes in circumstances.

SII Code of Conduct impact

Principle 1 – to act with integrity in fulfilling your responsibilities.

Principle 5 – to manage fairly and effectively, and to the best of your ability, any relevant conflict-of-interest.

Principle 7 – to strive to uphold the highest personal standards.

CUSTOMER RELATIONS

A client threatens to withdraw his business as a reaction against the standard wording on the foot of your firm's emails, which he feels is detrimental to his business.

BACKGROUND

You are a relationship manager at Knights, a well regarded boutique investment bank, where your director has been building a relationship with the finance director of Inks plc, a printing supplies manufacturer, for many months. Knowing that Inks has recently pulled out of a large acquisition deal, he believes that it is likely to be looking for another opportunity in the future.

Last week, this relationship building seemed to have paid off when Knights was approached by Inks plc and asked to tender for some corporate finance work. As ever, the time scale for producing the proposal document was tight, but the firm had been preparing for such an opportunity and seized it gratefully.

The team worked round the clock to produce the proposal document and yesterday it was finally sent to the finance director of Inks plc, using the firm's email system. All the members of the team are confident that the proposal should win, as the team includes a leading industry expert, has recently delivered a highly publicised and successful piece of work and your director has a good relationship with the finance director of Inks plc.

The engagement is expected to be highly lucrative and is vital to your team to reduce the possibility of redundancy, which is an ever present threat in today's difficult environment.

This morning, you were shocked when your director summoned you into his office and asked you to explain why the proposal document was sent to Inks plc in an email with a footer stating:

Our staff have chosen this year to support the charity Trees for Tomorrow.

'Is it really necessary to print this email – think before you print.'

You explained that the proposal was sent using a standard Knights email. Knights customises the footers of all its emails on a regular basis to promote various products and issues. For example, last quarter the footer promoted the ethical funds advisory service which Knights offers and read: 'Ethical funds – we can help you – think before you invest.'

You reminded him that the current footer had been given to Knights' staff to promote their chosen charity, which encourages environmental awareness, and currently all the firm's email footers read: 'Is it really necessary to print this email – think before you print'. You had not thought to remove the footer before sending the proposal.

Apparently, your director had received a rather irate telephone call from the finance director of Inks plc. The finance director had been offended by the footer, reminding your director that, as a leading manufacturer of printer inks, Inks' profits could be jeopardised if people took the footer seriously and reduced the amount of printing they performed. Your director had been told in no uncertain terms that, unless the footer was removed immediately from all Knights' emails, Knights' proposal would not be considered further.

Your director had indicated to Inks finance director that the email footers would be removed, noting that it was only a temporary footer anyhow. Your director asked you to determine who in the firm is responsible for the footers and to have it removed immediately.

Although you can understand the director's desire to appease Inks plc and so remain in the tender process, hopefully winning this highly lucrative piece of work, you can't help feeling that responding to a potential client in this manner is wrong and is, effectively, suggesting that the firm will do whatever it takes to win lucrative work.

You are conscious also that many of your colleagues, who support Knights' charitable initiatives and worked hard to get the bank to agree to use of the email footer, will be extremely angry if it is removed under these circumstances.

THE DILEMMA

If Knights changes the footer on its corporate emails in order to win the work:

- What impact will this have on Knights' reputation, which relies on the firm acting and being seen to act with complete integrity and objectivity?
- What message does this send to clients with regard to Knights' integrity and willingness to stand up for its beliefs?
- What would the bank's stakeholders think, given that Knights advertises its green credentials and currently has a high ranking in the Business in the Community index?
- What will be staff reaction to what might be regarded as outside interference in an internal matter, the firm's support for a charity chosen by the staff?

On the other hand, you could argue that:

- With the prospect of redundancies in the air this is no time to get defensive about such a seemingly trivial matter.
- Knights exists to make money and this will be a highly profitable potential client. Without the income which business such as Inks might provide, the bank would not be able to be so generous in its charitable support, nor employ so many staff.
- Changing the email footer is not a big deal – there are many other worthwhile messages that could be written instead.
- Footers are changed regularly and no-one else needs to know why the footer was changed a little earlier than normal.

OPTIMUM SOLUTION

The matter should be brought to the attention of the head of corporate finance so that an appropriate response can be discussed, hopefully defusing the situation.

Knights' reputation relies on it adhering to the highest standards of integrity and objectivity and, ideally, it should not accede to the demands of Inks plc by changing the offending footer.

Instead, it would be preferable for the head of corporate finance to explain the bank's position (and reason for the decision) to the finance director of Inks plc and seek to persuade him that the footer, on the one hand, and Knights' highly attractive proposal, on the other, should not be seen as incompatible. After all, inviting Knights to tender was presumably influenced, at least in part, by its reputation.

By standing up for its beliefs and explaining to Inks plc why it is reluctant to change the email footer, Knights should be able to maintain its reputation for integrity and trust. In essence, the question is the extent to which you or your firm should stand up for your own beliefs and policies and the extent to which you are prepared to dilute these in pursuit of commercial objectives.

However, it is pertinent to consider the impact which failure to win this mandate might have on staff numbers and, when faced with such a decision, staff might feel less hostile to the potential loss of the footer, the reason for its removal notwithstanding. Accordingly, it would be sensible to put the facts to the staff, so that they can be aware of the dilemma. Their response may be different in times when business is plentiful to when business opportunities are scarce.

In this instance, the trigger for this difficulty is something that is apparently quite trivial and the key to resolving it must be to ensure that it is not allowed to become more significant. Since appearing to give in, on the one hand, or losing the business on the other, might each be seen as a sign of failure, it is probably necessary to spend more time on resolving this issue than it might warrant in different circumstances and, if unavoidable, give in to the client, for the good of those staff members who might otherwise lose their job, having first made them aware of this possibility.

QUICK READ SUMMARY

CUSTOMER RELATIONS

What is/would be unethical

Immediately to give in to the threats of Inks plc, which, it can be argued, are themselves unethical. However, the overall decision must be a balance between what is ethically right under different circumstances, compared with what is right in today's difficult times. Arguably, therefore, the most ethical course of action is to consider the impact upon the employment prospects of your colleagues, should Knights fail to win the mandate because some staff insisted on standing up to Inks' threats and to act accordingly. However, it is important that the staff are made aware of the situation before a decision is made.

Key points summary

The corporate finance department of Knights is bidding for an important mandate from Inks plc.

Knights allows its staff to use its email footer to distribute a message supporting a charity of their choice. The current message urges people not to print emails, unless necessary, for environmental reasons.

Inks plc manufactures printing ink and feels that the message is inappropriate if Knights is to be its banker and demands that it is removed, failing which it will not do business with Knights.

Various members of staff feel that it is wrong to give in to threats of this nature.

If Knights does not win this mandate, a number of corporate finance staff may be made redundant.

Adverse consequences

There are two opposing sets of consequences in this dilemma.

On the one hand, there are the potential consequences of giving in to threats. While this is not a course of action which one would normally support, one must consider the particular circumstances. What Knights staff members are being asked to forgo is not significant in relation to the potential damage which might be caused by maintaining their position.

The opposite consequence is that the staff view prevails and a number of members of the corporate finance department lose their jobs, because Knights does not win the mandate.

Optimum approach

In this specific scenario the best outcome should leave both parties feeling happy with the outcome. That would be one in which, having explained to Inks plc the circumstances relating to the footer, ie, that it is a staff view, not the corporate view of Knights, and that it is only one of a regularly changing series of email footers, which will soon be replaced, Inks plc accepts what it is being told and withdraws its threat.

Nevertheless, Inks may be adamant and it is appropriate that your staff are made aware of the situation, and the possible consequences, before any irredeemable steps are taken.

Whether Knights wins the mandate, or not, can then be decided solely upon the merits of its proposal, without being influenced by seemingly irrelevant factors.

SII Code of Conduct impact

Principle 1 – to act honestly and fairly at all times when dealing with clients... be a good steward of their interests.

Principle 2 – to seek to avoid any acts which damage the reputation of your organisation.

Principle 3 – to observe professional conduct standards...and apply them according to principles rooted in honesty, trust and integrity.

A QUESTION OF DEGREE

Problems arise as a result of a failure properly to check the facts on the CV of a new recruit.

BACKGROUND

You are reviewing the performance assessments of a number of graduate trainees within your firm and also have been reading their CVs with a view to offering one of them a position in your department, as a part of their training.

The name of Tom catches your eye because he was a contemporary of your son's at school, before going on to a different university, from which he appears to have graduated successfully. He has received good reports from the various attachments that he has served and you feel that he would make a good addition to your team. However, because of the highly decentralised nature of the firm, you do not meet all of the trainees and have not seen Tom since your son introduced him briefly at a school function.

Consequently, the next time you speak to your son, you mention to him that Tom is now working in your firm and that he seems to have done well at university. Your son expresses surprise, saying that he had heard that Tom had dropped out of university after the second year to go travelling, following the death of his mother from cancer.

You advise your HR department of your interest in offering Tom an attachment in your team, but raise the issue of the apparent discrepancy in his CV and suggest that this is investigated.

After a few days a senior HR manager comes to see you to discuss Tom's CV and thanks you for bringing the matter to his attention. He says that there appears to have been a breakdown in procedures as Tom was offered a job on the graduate training scheme following employment, originally on a temporary basis, which had not required him to be a graduate. Consequently, Tom has been employed for the past year without complying with this requirement.

You are advised that this matter has now been pursued, as a result of which Tom has told HR that he is not able to produce the required certificate as he had not actually graduated. You are told by HR that Tom, at the end of his second year and following his mother's death, had been allowed to suspend his studies for a year and had left university with a view to spending a bit of time "clearing his head" but fully intending to resume his studies.

In the event, on returning from travelling and being short of money, Tom had started work as a temporary employee in a branch of your firm, telling HR that he had been at university before going travelling. Somehow this had been translated on Tom's file into his being awarded a degree and, after impressing the people with whom he worked, he was encouraged to apply for the firm's graduate training programme. After interview, he was accepted on to the programme and although, apparently, he was asked about his time at university, he was careful to avoid stating that he had graduated and maintains that he believed that everyone knew the true position.

THE DILEMMA

This situation appears to have arisen as a result of an internal error within the firm, although you get the impression that Tom was actually aware of this but did nothing to discourage the misconception. Accordingly, you are in something of a quandary as how best to proceed.

OPTIMUM SOLUTION

You feel that there are four potential courses of action open to you or the firm:

- You feel sympathetic towards Tom because of his personal loss and, since it was the firm's fault that it did not require him to produce his degree certificate, the current situation is of its making. Consequently, Tom's employment should be allowed to continue.
- You consider that Tom, although he has not been overtly dishonest, has not been as open and honest as a position with your firm requires. Therefore, regardless of the circumstances, and his good performance as a trainee, he should be asked to leave the firm.
- Tom was employed as a temp, without being required to have a degree. Because he has performed well and the firm is not blameless, he should be allowed to remain as a full time employee, but outside the graduate programme.
- Because of his good performance Tom should be offered the opportunity of remaining on the programme, subject to his completing his degree, within a specified time. This should also be accompanied by a freeze on his salary.

CONSIDERATIONS

There is a difference between exaggerating the importance of your position and resultant responsibilities on a CV and telling a deliberate lie. While putting the best gloss on your employment and education history is understandable, and because the actual role for which you are applying is unlikely to have been spelled out in detail, a degree of role/achievement inflation is, perhaps, inevitable. However, saying that you have achieved something or been awarded something which you have not, is dishonest.

Notwithstanding the above, you may feel sympathetic towards Tom's personal situation and because he was a school friend of your son, you may be tempted to take a more subjective view than otherwise you might. Nevertheless, if you simply allow his employment to continue it does send the wrong message about standards of honesty. And how might this decision be viewed by those people who actually have achieved the necessary qualifications and have not been offered a job? The most positive aspect is that Tom has performed very well at the jobs that he has been doing, but the fundamental point is that the judgment is about standards of honesty, not competence.

Alternatively, and it might be felt more appropriately, you judge Tom solely on his standard of honesty, which has been found wanting. Accordingly, you consider that the firm has no real option but to dismiss him. The fact that he is at an early stage in his working life should make much simpler his choice of what to do next, which might even include going back to university.

The option of allowing Tom to continue to work for the firm appears to be an attractive alternative, although it does duck the issue of whether you consider that Tom, in fact, has been dishonest. If that is considered to be the paramount issue, then this is not an option, but if the consensus view is that the firm is as much to blame as Tom, then this represents a reasonable compromise.

Finally, you may feel that Tom has shown the attributes necessary for a successful member of the graduate training programme and that he should be encouraged to continue his career with the firm. However, it would be inappropriate for this to be without some form of remedial action; in this case giving Tom time to complete his degree is an obvious option, although this might be difficult if he remains at work.

CONCLUSION

Clearly a degree of blame attaches to the firm, in that it has failed to adhere to its own procedures. Additionally, Tom has demonstrated that he can perform on a par with the other members of the graduate training scheme. However, his performance is not the main issue, which remains about standards of honesty. It may be felt that while Tom has not been actively dishonest, he appears to have done little or nothing to discourage the misconceptions about his degree status.

Therefore the most appropriate course of action is for the firm to tell Tom that he is unable to continue on the graduate training programme, but because of his satisfactory performance while on the programme, to offer him the alternative of continuing with the firm as a member of the mainstream staff.

QUICK READ SUMMARY

A QUESTION OF DEGREE

What is/would be unethical

In view of the circumstances, it would be unethical to take an extreme view in either direction, so that Tom is either treated over leniently or, conversely, the firm adopts a harsh line ignoring the degree of culpability on its own part.

Key points summary

A temporary employee, Tom, is invited to join the firm's graduate training programme in the mistaken belief that he has been awarded a degree.

Tom's CV says that he attended university.

HR department fails to check that Tom holds a degree.

He performs satisfactorily on the graduate programme.

You are considering offering Tom an attachment to your department.

You learn that Tom does not hold a degree.

Adverse consequences

To try to ignore the faults of either party would be wrong. Those within the firm who failed to check Tom's CV must be made aware of the problems that this has caused. Tom should understand that his economy with the truth also has consequences, both for himself and others, which could have been avoided.

Optimum approach

A course of action which recognises what Tom has achieved at the firm, while not ignoring the fact that he does not meet the requirements for the graduate training programme.

SII Code of Conduct impact

Principle 2 – to act with integrity in fulfilling the responsibilities of your appointment.

Principle 6 – to attain and actively maintain a level of professional competence appropriate to your responsibilities.

RECRUITMENT COMMISSION

A recruitment consultant offers to reduce his commission below his usual rates, provided that you make a payment to charity in addition to his firm's invoice.

BACKGROUND

A Far Eastern financial conglomerate is in the process of setting up a London-based broking subsidiary and you have been appointed head of human resources. The new CEO, who has just arrived from the Far East, has not worked before in London and is keen to begin operations as soon as possible. Although he possesses considerable broking experience, he is not familiar with the ways of the City of London, nor recruitment practice.

Your new CEO briefs you upon his business plan which requires the rapid hiring of a range of staff, including for a number of senior positions which will command substantial remuneration packages.

Given his inexperience in recruitment and in London, you explain to the CEO that it would be sensible to use the services of a recruitment consultant to find suitable staff, as this will speed up the process and also access candidates who may not easily be found if the firm handles the search itself.

You explain that there will be a significant commission payable to the consultant if he is successful in introducing candidates who are hired, but this has to be set against the costs of your firm placing advertisements, together with the considerable administrative burden of arranging and conducting all the initial screening interviews in-house.

Your CEO accepts your recommendation but indicates that while he is prepared to fund competitive remuneration packages, he wishes you to keep the recruitment consultancy fees as low as possible. You have developed excellent contacts in the recruitment /search industry and are due shortly to have lunch with John Smith, a partner in the small but very able consultancy, Williams, Green, Smith & Co, which you have used successfully in the past.

With these thoughts in mind you discuss the situation with John Smith over lunch. He is interested to hear about your new firm's urgent hiring needs and leaves you after the lunch saying that he will get back to you imminently. He telephones later the same day to put a proposition to you.

He offers, firstly, to reduce his normal commission from 30 per cent to 25 per cent of the agreed salary package. Additionally he suggests that, in view of your long-standing relationship, and outside the formally agreed terms, he will reduce his firm's invoice by a further 5 per cent, provided that you make a payment of half of this further reduction to a charity run by his wife, thus giving your firm an effective discount of 7.5 per cent on his firm's normal terms.

Having dealt with John Smith for some time, you are somewhat surprised at his proposal, but since he is not benefiting personally, you wonder what harm would be caused by taking advantage of this offer of an additional discount.

In support of the proposal, you consider the positive factors:

- You have previous satisfactory experience of using John Smith.
- Clearly he is keen to provide services to your firm on this occasion.
- He has offered to give you an attractive discount on his normal commission rate.
- Your firm will save a considerable amount of money on the anticipated costs.
- You will meet your CEO's requirement of keeping recruitment costs down.
- You will not benefit personally from any successful hiring.
- How the consultant choses to account for the income within his firm is of no concern to you.

You have not received an offer of this nature before and wonder how you should respond to the request for the allocation of the commission payment and whether it is actually any concern of yours. After all, you have not solicited this offer, it will not affect the quality of the candidates introduced and your firm will benefit from a further reduction in commission. Arguably, no-one loses and, in contemplating how to proceed, you wonder also whether it is really necessary to make your CEO fully aware of all aspects of this proposal.

OPTIMUM SOLUTION

You consider the possible courses of action:

- Simply go ahead with the proposal put to you by John Smith and keep the split commission arrangement between you and the accounts department. After all, there is nothing illegal in what you are doing and it appears to be to the benefit of your firm.
- Reject John Smith's proposal and walk away, advising your CEO that any proposal of this nature makes you feel uncomfortable, notwithstanding that there appears to be no obvious downside for your organisation.
- Check among your peers in other firms whether paying commission in this manner is common practice and be guided accordingly.
- Consider how comfortable you would be in having such a recruitment consultant working on behalf of your firm. What else might he be doing that he is not telling you about?
- As John Smith appears willing to accept a lower rate of commission, ask him to reduce his commission to the lower level.
- Advise your CEO of the full details of the consultant's offer and abide by his decision as to how the firm should proceed.

Having considered the various options, you decide that the appropriate course of action is to reject the offer of additional discount subject to your firm making a payment to charity on behalf of John Smith, but suggest that, while the extra discount is attractive to your firm, you can make payment as directed only on a formal invoice.

The argument that the request which is made is not uncommon practice in many situations is not a compelling reason for accepting it here, particularly if it makes you feel uncomfortable. While in a domestic situation the offer of a "discount for cash" is quite common, albeit that it may be ethically and legally dubious, it should not be used as an argument to support unusual, albeit apparently beneficial payment structures in a work context, where there appears no justifiable reason for such structures.

QUICK READ SUMMARY

RECRUITMENT COMMISSION

What is/would be unethical
It would be unethical to accept a greater level of fee reduction, subject to making a "side payment" to the charity nominated by John Smith, outside the terms of his invoice. Although you are not doing anything overtly dishonest, the structure of the payment does make you feel uncomfortable.

Key points summary
- You are recruiting personnel for a newly established London office of a Far East based bank.
- You intend to use the services of John Smith, a recruitment consultant known to you from previous engagements.
- John Smith offers you a discount on his firms "normal" rates of commission.
- He then offers you a further discount, subject to part of that reduction being paid to a third party, outside the terms of his firm's invoice.

Adverse consequences
Your greatest difficulty is perhaps that the proposed transaction gives you a feeling of unease. Although John Smith is a partner in the firm, you do not know the structure of the business and, thus, whether you are becoming a party to a fraud on the company, or its creditors.

Although what is requested has no obviously adverse consequences for you, or your employer, it does leave you feeling uncomfortable, even before you have discussed it with anyone else. Of itself that is an adverse feature in trying to ensure that you maintain the highest standards of integrity.

Optimum approach
Given your unease, the simplest and most appropriate course of action would be to use another recruitment agent. Alternatively, if you can respond without causing embarrassment on either side, then using John Smith, might be the most economical course of action, except for any lingering unease arising from John Smith's request.

SII Code of Conduct impact

The following principles are applicable to this situation:

Principle 2 – to act with integrity in fulfilling the responsibilities of your appointment.

Principle 5 – to manage fairly and effectively and to the best of your ability any relevant conflict of interest.

Principle 7 – to strive to uphold the highest personal standards including rejecting short term profits which may jeopardise your reputation.

REDUNDANCY

You are required to put forward names of colleagues for potential redundancy and are dismayed that this might include people with whom you have become friends.

BACKGROUND

You are a senior supervisor in a large financial services firm which, in common with many of its peers, has announced a significant number of redundancies and there is a generally unsettled feeling in the office.

You are approached by your line manager who tells you in confidence that he has been asked to review staff performance, with a view to implementing a 25 per cent across-the-board cut in staff numbers and he asks for your help in trying to identify staff whose names can be put on the list. The principal criterion is that their departure should not result in any operational problems.

This is a task in which you have always feared becoming involved, as you have built up your team over a number of years and, having encouraged them to think of themselves as more than just colleagues, have become friends with many of them. Consequently, it is seemingly inevitable that a number of your friends will find themselves on the list, regardless of whether or not you are responsible for their inclusion.

In preparation for the meeting to which you have been invited the following week, you consider all of your team individually and the more you look at their names, the more you are faced with the fact that almost all of them seem to have a reason, either personal or professional, why you do not want to put their names forward.

On the Tuesday night you spend a few wakeful hours wrestling with the problem of how to adopt a "professional" approach which will not leave you feeling that you have betrayed your colleagues and friends. Your mood is not helped when you get into the office early on Wednesday and Eddie, one of your team members, comes over and invites you for a lunchtime drink to celebrate the news that he and his wife Nicola are expecting their first child. Nicola used to be in your team, but now works in another part of the firm.

As Eddie says to you, the event is wonderful, but the timing could have been better, with all the uncertainty in the air about job security and he asks you whether you have heard anything on the grapevine. You reply that these are difficult times and that you are as concerned as everyone else.

At the meeting with the line manager, your HR manager is also present and says that the firm will need to ensure that all the appropriate procedures are followed as it doesn't want to get involved in claims for wrongful dismissal. The meeting starts with your line manager going through a list of members of staff who report to you, and making observations about the performance of a number of them, who he feels would not be a loss to the firm. Although you agree in general with his observations, which are based largely upon annual performance appraisals which you have signed, you are concerned when he mentions Eddie's name as being a possible contender for the list, bearing in mind what Eddie told you that morning.

The meeting ends and you are told that there will be a follow-up in a couple of days time to confirm the names. In the meantime, you have your lunchtime drink with Eddie to contend with and, although you think about trying to excuse yourself, you decide to go along as it would seem churlish not to, particularly since many other team members will also be there.

When you get to the pub Eddie buys you a drink and, while doing so, says that he had hoped that Nicola would be there, but her department has been summoned to a meeting and he is very worried that she might lose her job. At this point you wonder whether there is anything that you could say to Eddie to alert him to the possibility that he might suffer the same fate, or might you have a word with your line and HR managers?

THE DILEMMA

Understandably, you are concerned that a member of your staff may be about to lose his job at a time which is likely to be very stressful for him and his wife. This may be compounded if his wife also loses her job. You wonder whether there is anything that you could, or should, do to try to prevent this or to reduce its impact.

Should you intercede for personal reasons?

Should you try to soften the potential blow by tipping-off Eddie that he may be made redundant?

CONSIDERATIONS

When dealing with situations which have a direct human dimension, there is an obvious temptation to take actions which you might not otherwise take, particularly if you are friends with those involved. Accordingly, you may well ask yourself the questions:

Should I/Can I intercede for personal reasons? ie Eddie and his wife, who also works for the firm, are about to become parents.

Should I/Can I try to soften the potential blow, by tipping-off Eddie that he may be made redundant?

After all, there may be numerous other members of staff with situations which are much more difficult than Eddie is about to face, of which you are unaware. Should not you consider all of them as well? But how can you? And, if it is known that Eddie and his wife are being favoured, what might be the reaction of other members of staff? Alternatively, if you tip-off Eddie, how do you think that he might react?

OPTIMUM SOLUTION

When decisions have to be made that have a personal dimension, it is more important than ever to adhere to the primary requirements of ethical decision making and to measure your proposed course of action against the yardstick of openness, honesty, transparency and fairness.

In this instance, any overt action that you may be tempted to take to favour Eddie, however you to try to rationalise it, is likely to fall short of some or all of these requirements.

One consideration which, in a situation as personal as this, may not be at the forefront of your mind, is your responsibility to your firm, both as an entity and as a representative of the interests of all your other members of staff. Not only does this mean that you must seek to act objectively and impartially in this matter, but also that you have a primary responsibility towards your employer. This is a recurrent theme in the SII Code of Conduct, where it sits alongside your responsibilities to clients and the market.

Consequently, unless you have good business reasons, such as Eddie's performance being better than that of other potential nominees, or that he genuinely occupies a key role, you have no overriding reason for seeking to keep his name off the list.

Additionally, you may feel that you should tell HR that Eddie's wife is pregnant, but this is not a decision that you should make on Eddie's behalf. It is up to her and Eddie to decide who they will tell and when, even though this may have a bearing on the firm's decision on her future.

Accordingly, in this instance, the correct course of action must be to compile the list and then assess the strengths and weaknesses of all of the nominees. This would enable all of you involved in its compilation to consider matters objectively, before coming to a final list. It may be that this will actually result in Eddie being removed from the list but, even if it does not, you have acted in an ethical manner.

QUICK READ SUMMARY

REDUNDANCY

What is/would be unethical

It would be unethical to promote the interests of one member of staff over another, solely because of your personal friendship. It would also be unethical to divulge personal information to HR, even if you feel that you are doing the individual a favour. It would be unethical to tip-off Eddie.

Key points summary

Your firm is about to implement a redundancy programme.

One of your colleagues whom you supervise tells you that his wife is expecting a baby.

Your colleague's name is mentioned as a potential candidate for redundancy.

Adverse consequences

Although you may feel that there is no obvious adverse consequence for you in promoting the interests of one particular individual, your actions have to be measured against the yardstick of openness, honesty, transparency and fairness. The obvious loser is the member of staff who would lose their job because you have promoted a personal interest and thus you have compromised your integrity. The possibility exists also that when reviewing names of those to be made redundant, you are hard put to defend your colleague and then are forced to admit the reason why you have protected him. Dropping a hint to Eddie is also unacceptable and carries the hidden danger that you do not know how he might react. You assume that he will be grateful to you, but this may be a dangerous assumption.

Optimum approach

Your only sensible course of action is to do exactly what you are paid to do. Make recommendations as to which staff might be considered for redundancy on the basis of their performance. Management involves taking difficult decisions which may include actions involving friends, which on a purely personal basis you would not take.

If the opportunity occurs to discuss mitigating circumstances at a subsequent meeting, you will have the opportunity at that stage to raise the personal issues, provided that Eddie has advised HR by that time, or asked you to do so.

SII Code of Conduct impact

Principle 2 – to act with integrity in fulfilling the responsibilities of your appointment.

Principle 5 – to manage fairly and effectively, and to the best of your ability, any relevant conflict of interest.

Principle 7 – to strive to uphold the highest personal standards.

WEALTH MANAGER INCENTIVES

A new customer presents a tempting opportunity for an adviser to achieve his sales target and win a valuable incentive.

BACKGROUND

The Bank is a private bank that offers a range of its own investment products exclusively to its clients, who are mainly high net-worth individuals living in the UK. The Bank positions itself as a high quality "holistic" adviser and devotes considerable resources to maintaining a well-trained, competent, sales force. It prides itself on its exclusivity, the quality of its advisers and the fact that it offers innovative investment products to its private clients.

The Bank's compliance department has, in conjunction with senior management and the product development team, imposed relatively tight restrictions on the sale of these funds, as they only have quarterly liquidity, and they are valued only after any sales or purchases have been made. Advisers have to demonstrate that any proposed investment does not exceed a certain proportion of the client's overall investments and also to demonstrate that the potential client has alternative liquidity available, in the event that they may not be able to realise their investment.

As demand for these funds has increased, more and more pressure has been applied by The Bank's advisers, and by the product development team, to relax the restrictions and over time they have been loosened. Now, The Bank's senior management, convinced that hedge funds sales are a way to encourage clients to stay with the firm and also to provide a good source of "upfront" income to the firm, is demanding more and more sales from The Bank's advisers.

Advisers' compensation has always taken the form of a salary and performance-related bonus, but following a recent takeover, everyone has been repapered. The incentive structure has been changed to a lower basic but higher results-based compensation and there is a suspicion amongst some observers and staff that this has led to a lowering of standards.

The Bank's management now uses competitions and league tables to incentivise its employees, and by "naming and shaming" those advisers who are not "stepping up to the plate". The advisers who make the biggest sales are rewarded with high-profile weekend breaks; those who fail to make their targets are publicly identified.

Following the introduction of the incentives, advisers have sought to put more and more of their clients' money into the funds and capacity has been reached in several of the existing funds. As a result, The Bank's product development team has created more and more funds, with increasingly esoteric strategies and The Bank's compliance department is expected to relax the guidelines for clients' exposure to hedge funds.

The advisers, faced with another competition that will see ten of them sent on an all-expenses paid trip to the Monaco Grand Prix, and with an eye on the 'league table' that has just been published on the Bank's intra-net, are preparing to promote The Bank's 'BRIC' Long/Short fund to their private clients.

Henry has been an adviser with The Bank for five years and has always been considered to be in the top half of the performance table. He has been told by his manager that he is expected to put £10m of client money into the new fund. Although a number of his existing clients have purchased every fund that has been launched to date, currently he is struggling to make his target and his manager has expressed disappointment, telling Henry that The Bank expects more, adding that he is letting down the whole team.

The Bank's senior management believes that it is on to a winner with its hedge funds and the parent company is delighted with the income that The Bank is now providing. How can they stop themselves from getting carried away with this strategy, if indeed they should?

THE DILEMMA

Henry goes to a meeting with a new potential client, who has a substantial inheritance of £2m to invest, but apparently has little investment knowledge, and Henry considers it unlikely that the client would say no to a persuasive argument. Henry is keen to win a place on the trip to Monaco and has the presentation for the 'BRIC' Long/Short Fund on his laptop.

Henry meets the customer and his preconceptions regarding his investment knowledge are confirmed when the customer says that he has heard a lot about hedge funds, and friends have told him that they are the way to make money, so he wants to invest heavily in them.

What should Henry do? This could be just what he needs to help him on his way to Monaco.

OPTIMUM SOLUTION

There are a number of considerations, some of which relate to matters governed by rules and others where such considerations do become very much a grey matter.

The majority of readers will be familiar with the test of "suitability" when recommending investments to clients but this cannot be an exact science. In this instance, the suggestion has been made that a "persuasive argument" should win the day for Henry, but what does this mean? It could mean that Henry talks his client into making an investment which, had the client really understood the features, he would not have made. That would clearly be a potential recipe for trouble, the client's enthusiasm notwithstanding.

Alternatively, it could mean that Henry really understood the product, which he explained clearly to his client and his client made a decision based on the facts presented. It may not have been a very good investment decision, but it was the client's.

Henry has a number of options, but none of these may be the answer that both The Bank and Henry are looking for:

i) "Sell" the investment and persuade the customer to take the maximum amount consistent with his firm's more robust policy, and document the appropriate "know your customer" information in order to demonstrate that this was the client's decision.

ii) Recommend a significant, but proportionate, investment in the specified product, but not to the exclusion of other appropriate asset classes and in line with the customer's profile.

iii) Sign up the customer but do not make the investment. Recommend risk free investments with a view to reviewing in six months' time.

iv) Discuss with his boss his concerns about the stretching targets that are being set, in relation to products which are becoming increasingly exotic.

Henry could well take course of action i), particularly given the incentive on offer and the encouragement of his employer, although at the back of his mind he clearly has some concerns. If he does this, he will have to be careful to document all that transpires so that the client cannot subsequently claim that he was being misled. However, the question remains whether such an approach is ethical. Ignoring the incentives, either of ii) or iii) would be preferable, albeit that iii) might be regarded as overly cautious.

If Henry does not believe that the product is right for his client, and does not conform to The Bank's policy, he should be careful to document his reasons, and resign himself to the fact that any trip that he might make in the near future is unlikely to be to Monaco.

In this instance The Bank and its decision chain appear to have taken a conscious decision that the product has wide appeal and can safely be marketed without any apparent caveats or health warnings to clients. However, your compliance department has not yet formally confirmed that the looser terms still meet regulatory requirements. Even in the absence of this confirmation it would be a bold adviser who felt able to allow such a significant opportunity to pass by, when promotion of the product apparently has official support.

However, the financial climate is now much more risk averse and banks are less keen on an aggressive, sales-target driven approach than previously was the case.

QUICK READ SUMMARY

WEALTH MANAGER INCENTIVES

What is/would be unethical

The Bank launches a new product of a type where sales had been closely controlled. Now it wants the new product sold more widely and is incentivising its staff with a mixture of rewards, together with implicit threats if targets are not met. The compliance department has not yet signed off unequivocally on this less rigid policy. From the perspective of the firm's policy makers, it is unethical to put more junior staff in the position of being offered incentives, accompanied by implicit threats, if it encourages them to suspend their usual ethical standards. From a sales perspective it is unethical to recommend an investment to a client which is more to your benefit than to the customer.

Key points summary

The Bank incentivises sales staff using competitions to reward successful performers.

At the same time, it publishes details of those who have failed to meet their sales targets.

Henry is in a quandary as to how much he might compromise his principles to meet his targets.

The Bank appears not to share Henry's concerns about suitability of the investment product.

Adverse consequences

Appearing to persuade customers to invest in a product which they do not understand, and which may not serve their best interests, is leaving the adviser, and his employer, open to accusations of misselling and failing to treat customers fairly. The fact that there are additional incentives for making sales only makes matters worse, should the investment not perform as anticipated.

Optimum approach

This must be to consider that your customer's interests are paramount, ignoring the effect that this may have on your sales targets. If you can satisfy your customer, as well as achieving your sales target, this is a bonus, but it must not be your main consideration.

SII Code of Conduct impact

Principle 1 – to act honestly and fairly at all times when dealing with clients.

Principle 2 – to act with integrity ...avoid any acts...which damage the reputation of your organisation.

Principle 3 – to observe applicable professional conduct standards.

Principle 5 – to manage fairly and effectively...any relevant conflict of interest.

Principle 7 – to strive to uphold the highest personal standards.

case studies 7-12

for the more experienced practitioner

autocrat

proprietary information

global standards

a matter of reputation

creative accounting

world tour

AUTOCRAT

A new chief executive introduces a strategy which causes you to have serious concerns about the future of the firm. How might you deal with this?

BACKGROUND

You work as risk director in a large firm of financial advisers and report directly to the chief executive, as well as being a member of the executive committee, which includes the chief executive, the sales director and the finance director.

After many years during which your firm has gained a reputation as a solid and reliable, albeit rather staid operator, a new high profile chief executive with a non-financial background and a reputation as a demanding task-master takes over, and begins to change the focus and culture of the firm. The chief executive now seeks much higher levels of performance and in an attempt to achieve this, initiates a large increase in the sales force, where the accent is on proven sales success, regardless of the product, rather than financial awareness.

At the same time your firm begins to promote financial products from a wider variety of providers, offering more complex products to existing clients and gaining new clients attracted by the apparently higher returns. At the same time a number of the more experienced advisers are encouraged to leave the firm for not buying-in to the new environment and being unable to accept the new sales driven culture that now prevails.

While you observe these moves as being in the nature of the business environment, you have concerns that the increased risks which will result from this change in the focus of the business are not being fully advised to the board. Although the initial impact of the changes is almost entirely positive, with significant increases in client numbers and income being generated by the expanded sales force, there are disquieting signs that the improvement is not entirely risk-free.

You run a major programme of customer feedback and receive several thousand feedback forms each year, which are analysed monthly. Historically, the forms have shown high levels of customer satisfaction in nearly all categories and your firm performs very well against its peers in industry surveys. Indeed, two years ago, you won an industry award for customer loyalty.

However, the feedback forms are now much less consistently good and the trend over the last six months is downwards in most of the key areas of customer satisfaction. Additionally you have received reports of disquiet from a number of older clients at what they consider to be the high-pressure tactics now being employed. Consequently you prepare a note for discussion at the next executive committee reporting this disquiet and suggesting that some tempering of the programme might be considered, to enable remedial action to be taken to restore the firm's standing and to ensure that you do not attract the attention of the regulator.

When the executive committee meets, your note is the last agenda item and the chief executive makes it clear that he does not consider it a major issue, saying that the sales figures speak for themselves and he has had no complaints from the finance director about the firm's increased income. The sales director, who was appointed by the chief executive, supports him saying that while it is obviously disappointing that client satisfaction has slipped, until it starts to affect financial performance it is not something he is concerned about. In any case the firm's satisfaction rating remains comparable with peer-group firms and ruffling a few feathers just shows that the sales teams are trying hard. The chief executive adds that this is an acceptable price to pay for the extra effort that must be made to recover ground that the firm lost by failing to respond to changes in the market and adds that he is fully behind the sales team's performance. The chief executive reminds you that profits are 36 per cent up, the share price has increased by 29 per cent and the executive share options, some of which have been awarded to you, vest in three months at a significant 72 per cent premium.

However, you are disappointed that your concerns have not been taken seriously, to the extent that the minutes of the meeting mention the discussion only under the heading of "any other business-statistical presentation" and your unease is not diminished when the next set of feedback forms continues the downward trend. At the same time, your firm is the subject of two customer complaints to the ombudsman, which has never happened previously. You again raise the subject at the executive committee and again your concerns are brushed aside, the sales director commenting that the industry as a whole is getting more complaints than hitherto, so you are not alone.

You become increasingly frustrated at what you perceive to be a blind disregard of some obvious risks, but at this stage feel that you are taking all the steps that you can to bring your concerns to the attention of the firm's executive. However, your disquiet increases significantly when you learn that Shamrock, one of the providers of a product that your firm has heavily promoted, has announced that it is limiting redemptions, as a result of which your advisers are being deluged with calls from worried clients. Many of these are extremely hostile and talking about taking legal action against your firm.

You now believe that, as risk director, you must report this matter to the board and once again raise your overall concerns with the executive committee, highlighting this latest turn of events. You support this concern with figures showing the rising level of complaints and your firm's diminishing position in the various media surveys in which you figure. You also compile figures showing the value to the firm's income stream of Shamrock's products and identify others with similar characteristics, which may be subject to the same restrictions, or where sales are likely to dry up on client concern. You add that you believe that you should stop promoting them, which would additionally affect your income.

The chief executive, angrily and publicly tells you that he is disappointed that you seem determined to focus only on the negative aspects of the firm's performance, and that while he understands your concerns, he believes that you are exaggerating them and he has no intention of involving the board in the minutiae of day-to-day operating issues. He considers that the firm remains in good shape and that any fall-off in sales will be recovered through the hiring of further sales advisers. There is silence after the chief executive has spoken. A few moments later, the finance director, who was promoted by the chief executive, says that he also is confident that any financial fall-out from Shamrock will be more than covered by income from the sale of new products. No-one else says anything and you feel uncomfortable at continuing the topic.

THE DILEMMA

- As risk director you believe that there are serious risks to your firm that other executives, mindful that they owe their position to the chief executive, are unwilling properly to consider.
- You strongly believe that the board should be made aware of these risks and advised of the steps that are being taken to mitigate them.
- You are concerned that the chief executive is focusing exclusively on headline performance, without wanting to consider the risks to the firm in achieving it.

CONSIDERATIONS

- You have shared your concerns with the chief executive through the appropriate channel.
- You believe that because your message is unwelcome, it is being ignored.
- The minutes of the committee meeting, although reporting the discussions, have been written to put a different slant on what was said.
- If you go above the chief executive, you are going against him. Therefore, you are likely to have only one opportunity to get your message across.
- Failure to have your concerns accepted will seriously undermine your position and possibly leave you with resignation as your only sensible option.
- The current economic climate is harsh and you will lose your share options.

THE WAY FORWARD

Given that you will have only one chance of success, you need to speak out and escalate this matter to the senior independent director (SID).

You will need to seek a private meeting with him, which would be more appropriate on neutral ground to enable you to present your case without the danger of the chief executive being called in to challenge your version of events. Assuming that the SID has an office elsewhere, it would be advisable to try to meet there.

It is essential that you provide the SID with a carefully, documented train of events, supported by an objective presentation of the information that you have supplied to the executive committee, setting out your reasoning and the responses that you received.

At this stage, speaking to the regulator is not an appropriate course of action, given that you have not exhausted the internal avenues available to you, but this must be an option if the SID is dismissive of your report. However you should be prepared to accept that once your report has been given a fair and considered hearing at the appropriate level, which so far it has not, the board view may not coincide with yours.

That being the case, resignation may be your only option and you should review your motivation before taking any external "whistleblowing" options. Is this simply a commercial disagreement, or is there a "public interest" aspect, which would provide you with protection in terms of the Public Interest Disclosure Act?

Similarly, you must accept that even if the SID supports you, you will need his protection. Internal relationships within the firm are not going to be the same. It is probable that you will need at least to move roles, so that you do not have the same reporting lines and, possibly, to look for another job, notwithstanding that whistleblowing legislation requires that the firm does not discriminate against you.

The SID also has a difficult choice, as supporting you means going against the chief executive, whose recruitment he may have overseen, so the stakes are high.

At the end of the day, you may be forced to accept that you are in a minority over this issue, but if you are able to offer a properly argued and presented point of view, then acting with integrity requires that you take this step, while being mindful of the possible consequences.

QUICK READ SUMMARY

AUTOCRAT

What is/would be unethical

If you have serious concerns about the impact on the company of the present strategy, it would be wrong not to ensure that your concerns are heard at the highest level.

It is equally wrong of the chief executive to try to sweep your concerns under the carpet. You are the risk director and, as such, it is your job to ensure that these matters are properly considered.

Key points summary

You are the risk director in a firm in which a new chief executive has embarked on a new sales focused strategy.

Although the sales strategy is working well, you are concerned about the impact that it is having on the firm's hard earned reputation. You are concerned also about the sustainability of the strategy in the light of problems with a specific product.

The chief executive does not accept your concerns and does not relay them to the board. In fact he seeks to have them minimised in the company's internal records.

Adverse consequences

Whether you do, or do not, take further action may have adverse consequences for you.

If you take no further action, continued pursuit of the chief executive's sales strategy will result in further erosion of the firm's reputation which may then begin to impact on sales, thus creating a vicious circle.

Raising the level of your concerns with board members also has potential adverse consequences for you, either if you do not receive their support, but also potentially if you do.

Optimum approach

Having ensured that you have followed company policy scrupulously and fully documented all that you have done, escalate the matter to the senior independent director. You should be prepared to accept that your view may still not be accepted, in which case you will have to decide whether you remain convinced of your views, at which point you should raise your own concerns with the regulator.

SII Code of Conduct impact

Principle 2 – to act with integrity in fulfilling the responsibilities of your appointment.

Principle 3 – to observe applicable professional conduct standards ...

Principle 5 – to manage fairly and effectively any relevant conflict of interest ...

Principle 7 – to strive to uphold the highest personal standards, including rejecting short-term profits.

PROPRIETARY INFORMATION

You discover that an executive who you recruited has helped your firm win business using material acquired from a competitor. The source of this material is no longer available, so do you need to take any further action?

BACKGROUND

You are the chief executive of Talpa, an industrial consultancy business. It has hired a new finance director from the specialised industry group, Bravo, a global firm of consultants, which is acknowledged as being among the leaders in its field.

The position of finance director is a key appointment in your strategy to grow your consultancy and your appointment of Stephan to the position seems to be paying dividends. Stephan oversees your tender process for a key piece of new business and you are impressed with his proposals, which are both well structured and detailed, including a lot of supporting material to justify his recommendations.

Accordingly, when your firm is awarded the mandate in the face of stiff competition, including from Bravo, you feel vindicated in your choice of Stephan, who was not universally well received in some quarters.

A continuous flow of new business is required to support your expansion plan and Stephan plays a major role in ensuring that Talpa's bids are competitive, both on price and structure.

Stephan's approach continues to pay off and your success rate in the bids which your firm makes for new business improves from about 40 per cent to 75 per cent, which you ascribe largely to Stephan's focused approach. Consequently you ask him to institute an internal training programme for the more junior members of the firm to make use of his skills.

Following the first session, your PA tells you how impressed he was with the training and says, jokingly, that the vital ingredient seems to be to know what your competitors are doing. While agreeing with this sentiment you say that is clearly what everyone would like to be able to do, but at Talpa you have to rely on more conventional methods.

After a successful 12 months, Stephan asks you for special leave, telling you that his brother is terminally ill and he wishes to help his sister-in-law, who is finding life difficult. You agree that Stephan should take his annual leave and extend it so that he will be away for at least a month, during which time you will oversee his team.

Stephan has been away for only a week when his assistant Laura, who is now overseeing your firm's latest consultancy bid, tells you that she is hampered because she has no access to most of Stephan's papers from Talpa's previous bids which, apparently, Stephan uses as the basis for his new tenders. Laura tells you that she has phoned Stephan but was able only to leave a message with his wife.

Later that day Laura tells you that she has found some of Stephan's papers in his desk, which had been locked, but to which she had found a key. She says that these will be useful but she is surprised that among them are copies of slides with the Bravo logo on them. Immediately you are concerned at the possible implications and ask to see the papers. However, you are relieved when you see that they are industry reports published by Bravo, which are openly available.

In due course Stephan telephones and you tell him that you have opened his desk, but that it was not helpful that the most useful parts of his working papers appeared to be elsewhere and that all that you had found were some Bravo slides. On learning that his desk had been opened Stephan becomes agitated, saying that it contained only private papers and that he would bring the documents that he had at home to the office the next day.

Stephan comes into the office as arranged with two briefcases full of files and apologises profusely for having kept them at home and also his reaction on learning that his desk had been opened. You thank him for bringing back the files and, after discussing his brother's worsening condition, Stephan leaves and you pass the files to Laura.

The following day Laura comes to see you saying that she has been through the files, which are very helpful, containing as they do a number of references to Bravo's figures and plans, which had enabled Talpa to structure its proposals in a way that enabled the firm to win a number of mandates.

You are alarmed at the implications and, notwithstanding Stephan being on leave, you decide that you must speak with him. You get through to Stephan's wife, who tells you that his brother has died and that he is at his sister-in-law's house, so you simply leave a message asking that Stephan call you as soon as he feels able. It is two days before Stephan telephones and you ask him to come to the office as you have an important issue to discuss, which needs him to be present.

In the meantime you consider the implications of what you have in your files. Whatever the explanation, you appear to have proprietary information which is the property of a competitor and it looks as though Talpa has made use of it to the benefit of the firm.

When Stephan returns to the office he immediately asks to see you and says:

"Clearly I owe you an explanation".

HOW WOULD YOU RESPOND?

The first point must be to establish how the information that you have in your file came to be there and you ask Stephan for an explanation.

Stephan tells you that before joining Talpa both he and his brother worked for Bravo and when he left the firm he had no intention of taking anything beyond the experience that he had gained. Clearly there were some things that he would remember, but he made no conscious decision to take information. However, one weekend Stephan visited his brother, who was working on a Bravo bid and as Stephan was leaving, his brother gave him his presentation saying "you might like to have a look at this!" Stephan appreciated that this was not something that he should be doing, but convinced himself that he would just have a quick look at the papers and then shred them. Unfortunately the proposals were quite complicated and to understand them fully Stephan had to spend some time studying the papers which he then kept at home.

After Talpa won the bid his brother continued to send him information from Bravo and Stephan told himself that as he had received the information, he might as well use it principally to the benefit of Talpa, and only indirectly to himself.

Clearly, since his brother had now died, the source of this information was no longer available, so this would not happen again. Stephan said that he recognised what he had done was wrong and apologised for putting you in this position.

OPTIMUM SOLUTION

You may consider that since this is a situation which appears to have come to a natural conclusion, you will accept the obvious temptation and say, "you resign and we shall forget all about it". The question is whether allowing Stephan to resign is adequate. However, if you decide that it is not, what might you do, and what might be the impact on Talpa?

A simple thought might be that you should own up to Bravo, in the expectation that, because the source of the information had died, the company would respond in a restrained way and take the view that it is "water under the bridge".

But there is a danger that Bravo, having lost a number of contracts to Talpa, which appear to be directly as a result of the "theft" of information, may feel that it should take legal action to have Talpa disgorge the profits generated from these contracts, possibly also seeking damages. Such an action might be the end of Talpa as a firm and, even if the specific outcome of the litigation does not result in irreparable financial damage to Talpa, consequent reputational damage may prove terminal.

Nevertheless, the ethical course of action must be to open a dialogue with Bravo, advising the firm of what has occurred. Clearly you should seek to establish that Farma won the mandates as a result of its own work, but accept that is likely to be strongly disputed and a compromise may be required if you are to avoid litigation.

Then there is the question of how you deal with Stephan. Obviously he cannot stay, but should you accept his resignation or sack him? Given the serious nature of this situation, and that he has been with Talpa for a relatively short time, there is no reason for consideration of any course of action other than dismissal.

QUICK READ SUMMARY

PROPRIETARY INFORMATION

What is/would be unethical

It is unethical to use proprietary information, however it comes in to your possession and having used it, albeit unwittingly, not then to tell the owners of it.

Key points summary

Your new finance director seems to provide the firm with a vital commercial edge.

The firm wins a greater proportion of competitive bids than before he joined.

During the finance director's absence from the office it is revealed that he has possession of valuable proprietary information of a competitor.

The finance director admits that he was given the information by his brother, who has since died.

Although the source of the information is no longer available, action should be taken to tell the owners of the information.

Adverse consequences

Because this situation will not recur, your first reaction may be that no external action is necessary and your only problem, if any, is the future of the finance director.

Advising Bravo that you have used their information may result in serious financial and reputational damage to Talpa.

Saying nothing may seem an attractive option, but should leave you wrestling with your conscience.

Optimum approach

Tell the owners of the information that you have been given it and, unknown to you, the firm made use of it.

You will have to deal appropriately with the finance director and the correct course of action must be dismissal, since he was fully aware of his actions and their possible consequences.

SII Code of Conduct impact

Principle 1 – to act honestly and fairly at all times ...

Principle 2 – to act with integrity in fulfilling your responsibilities ...

Principle 3– to observe applicable law, regulations and professional conduct standards ...

Principle 7 – to strive to uphold the highest personal standards, including rejecting short-term profits which may jeopardise your reputation and that of your employer.

GLOBAL STANDARDS V PROFITABILITY

Differing global standards of disclosure give you the opportunity to promote a new investment fund in a number of countries where lower standards of disclosure are required than in your home country.

BACKGROUND

You are the marketing director of a UK-based international fund management group which provides a range of collective funds, sold mainly in the UK and Europe, where increasing competition has required ever greater marketing efforts and the development of innovative, new fund offerings.

One such new fund invests in high-tech companies located in, and serving, developing nations. The fund managers use some innovative derivative techniques to leverage performance, which has been very promising, although rather volatile.

As a result of UK regulatory requirements, detailed disclosure has been necessary in marketing and sales literature, in order to inform potential investors of the significant risks, including the volatility, to which the fund is subject. You consider that these explicit disclosures have constrained sales of what, you are advised, is an inherently sound fund.

The group has no global standards covering this type of situation and the policy of your group is that each group company must comply with the laws and regulations of the country in which it operates.

Faced with increasing competition and stringent regulatory requirements within the UK and EU, one of your team suggests that this high-tech fund be promoted, via your Asian subsidiaries, to potential investors in countries in that region where regulatory requirements are less demanding.

On researching this idea, you find that there are several countries in the region where there appears to be growing demand for similar investments and where the local regulatory requirements do not require specific disclosure of the degree of risk or of the likely volatility of the fund. Furthermore, you ascertain that in two of these particular countries there is no equivalent to the UK Financial Services Compensation Scheme.

An additional attraction of the fund is that it invests in a number of high-tech companies, which are located in the region where you are considering targeting your promotion.

Your research also reveals that one of your principal competitors has enjoyed recent success in promoting one of its funds in this region, without any apparent problems arising from regulators or investors. Their fund seems to be relatively high risk, but this factor is not prominent in their marketing literature.

This seems to present an attractive marketing opportunity and you wonder whether you should take advantage of it, and how you might do so.

FACTORS TO CONSIDER

In favour of increased promotional and sales activity are:
- This is an inherently sound fund in a region where there is growing demand and where the fund invests directly.
- There are no legal or regulatory requirements upon your subsidiary to make the detailed risk and volatility disclosures that may have hindered marketing in the UK.
- There are no investor compensation arrangements to worry about.
- A competitor appears to be enjoying success without any problems.

On the other hand:
- Benign regulatory requirements in the region might change.
- The volatile performance of the fund means that the possibility of loss, as well as profit, by investors is higher than is normally acceptable.
- Foreign investors would be treated less favourably than home state investors.
- In the event of unsophisticated investors incurring losses as a result of investing in this unrestricted fund, there might be a significant public backlash.
- Such a situation might damage your group's reputation.

OPTIMUM SOLUTION

Your first consideration might be whether it is actually ethical for your group selectively to adopt weaker local legal/regulatory requirements, rather than the higher standards required in your home country.

Should it be a matter for each subsidiary board as to the level at which it sets its ethical standard?

In the event that the fund loses money, and your firm considers that it is in its interests to compensate UK investors, notwithstanding the risk warning given, would you be comfortable that a less generous approach is taken towards investors in a different regulatory environment?

To what extent should your recommendation be influenced by the fact that a competitor, possibly with less rigorous standards, is taking advantage of a particular situation.

RECOMMENDATION

For a group with international or global representation, the absence of a group-wide standard can be corrosive of standards generally, which are likely to gravitate towards acceptance of the lowest standard that can be got away with.

However, when devising group standards, it should be recognised that the standards accepted in the "home" state are not necessarily the "best," and higher standards may apply elsewhere. Additionally, there may be a distinction between your group's minimum acceptable commercial standards and regulatory requirements.

Accordingly, by adopting the positions that firstly, a minimum group standard should apply and secondly, this should require the adoption of the higher of local standards or minimum group standards, the answer in this case would be that investors overseas should be subject to the same protections as are offered to UK investors, notwithstanding that the opportunity exists to adopt lower standards.

QUICK READ SUMMARY

GLOBAL STANDARDS V PROFITABILITY

What is/would be unethical

Your firm promotes and manages an overseas investment fund with quite a high level of volatility and which carries a higher than normal level of risk.

It would be unethical to take advantage of lower standards of disclosure, to the potential detriment of overseas investors, if it resulted in them receiving less favourable treatment in the event of a problem with the fund than investors in your home country.

Key points summary

Your firm has offices around the world.

It does not have group-wide standards of business conduct and integrity.

It operates a higher risk fund, that invests in overseas businesses.

You have the opportunity to promote the fund overseas, taking advantage of different standards of disclosure in a number of overseas countries

Due to the degree of risk, investor compensation in the event of problems with the fund is one of your considerations.

Should you be influenced by the fact that overseas jurisdictions may have lower standards than your home state?

Adverse consequences

The most serious consequences are reputational damage and incurring the attention of the regulator for applying differing standards of behaviour towards investors in the same product, but who are covered by the rules of different jurisdictions. Not only might this apply to your behaviour in relation to this specific product but it might also have a knock-on effect into other parts of your organisation, which have no connection with the original problem.

Optimum approach

The fact that you are able to do something does not mean that you should do it, or that it is the right thing to do. Consequently, there is no justification for offering different terms to investors in the same product, simply because they are covered by regulatory jurisdictions with varying requirements. Accordingly, if you decide that you will promote the fund overseas it should be on the basis of investors receiving the same level of information and protection as those in your home state.

The next step should be the examination of group policies to see where there are significant differences in the application of standards between different jurisdictions and consideration by the board whether it is happy for the group to operate in this way.

SII Code of Conduct impact

Principle 1 – to act honestly and fairly at all times when dealing with clients...

Principle 2 – to act with integrity in fulfilling your responsibilities...

Principle 3 – to observe applicable law, regulations and professional conduct standards ... according to principles rooted in trust, honesty and integrity.

Principle 7 – to strive to uphold the highest personal standards, including rejecting short-term profits which may jeopardise your reputation and that of your employer.

A MATTER OF REPUTATION

You have concerns about whether a potential valuable customer will prove to be an asset, or whether his uncertain history may cause problems in the future.

BACKGROUND

You are the chief executive of the wealth management division of a traditional UK merchant bank. Results and profitability have been disappointing recently as a result of ever increasing competition from US and European rivals who adopt a more aggressive, and possibly less risk-averse approach to business, than does your own institution.

The board has charged you with reinvigorating the wealth management business in order to increase profitability, which you are keen to do, but are unsure as to whether the bank's traditional, conservative attitude to risk has really changed.

The bank has recently hired from a competitor a new client relationship director, Bruce, who has good connections in Suburbia, an oil rich, independent state which was formerly a constituent part of the USSR.

Bruce mentions to you the prospect of taking on a new client, Alexander, whom he has known for a number of years through the relationship at his previous bank. Alexander is an ultra high net worth client and has made his money from the supply of equipment to the Suburbian oil industry. There is the prospect of the early deposit of £25m, with substantially more to follow, and the establishment of a full discretionary investment management mandate, including the possibility of providing a range of ancillary services.

You are told that if Alexander is successfully taken on by the bank, there is a good prospect that further clients may follow who are known to him. Given your remit from the board, by taking on Alexander together with the prospect of further clients, you can envisage substantially increased profitability for your division.

In view of the board's conservative attitude to reputational risk, you speak with your compliance officer who recommends that a report is commissioned from a risk intelligence firm, which specialises in probing the background of wealthy and high profile individuals.

You agree to this course of action and a week later the report is delivered. It indicates that Alexander has, in the past, been the subject of some negative comment and rumour within Suburbia concerning the origins of his wealth and there is speculation that he may have been involved in the bribery and corruption which remains a feature of the business environment in that country.

Alexander was convicted of a bribery charge six years ago but has no other criminal convictions and all of the unfavourable comment and rumour ceased shortly after that time. Among Alexander's supporters there are suggestions that this charge may have been fabricated by the authorities. Subsequently Alexander successfully sought asylum in the UK. For over five years there have been no negative comments and more recently he has received a number of favourable press reviews concerning his services to industry and employment in the UK.

On questioning the risk intelligence firm about its findings, it indicates to you that this situation is not untypical; the further back you research very wealthy individuals from this part of the world, the more likely you are to find some suggestions of impropriety, seldom supported by hard evidence. In more recent years, such individuals, having amassed their wealth, have led apparently blameless lives.

Indeed, Alexander has recently been receiving very favourable mention from politicians and the UK media, as a result of establishing significant employment opportunities within his growing business empire, much of which is situated in areas of high unemployment in the UK. A further, large financial investment is soon to be made by him within the constituency of the Prime Minister, which will create many hundreds of new jobs, as well as providing new facilities for local youth and old people. The media has wondered whether Alexander might be in line for some sort of honour as a result of his good works

You are due to hold a new account opening committee meeting, at which decisions are made on whether or not you take on potential new accounts, and the risk intelligence report will be circulated to all committee members beforehand. The committee consists of Bruce, who will almost certainly vote in favour of taking on this client, your compliance officer, who has told you that in view of the report he will probably vote against the proposal, and yourself. Accordingly, you are likely to have the casting vote.

What would you do?

THE CONSIDERATIONS

At a fundamental level, the question is whether the potential benefit from having Alexander as a client is likely to outweigh any potential "embarrassment" which might result, should it turn out that he is, in fact, operating in a manner which discredits his high profile status in the UK.

On the positive side, in favour of accepting this business is the fact that your intelligence report does not reveal any current problems between Alexander and the existing regime in Suburbia. Equally, it is a reasonable assumption that before embracing him too warmly, government departments have carried out similar research to your own which, presumably, has not uncovered more than your own investigations, although such research is not infallible and government may have taken different considerations into account. Consequently you might feel that there is no overpowering reason why you should not take advantage of this opportunity.

You are not being asked to deal with the government of Suburbia but with an individual who appears hostile to the current regime and may have business and personal dealings which are designed to undermine it. However, you do not have evidence of this.

On the negative side is the fact that your report does not give Alexander a clean bill of health and there must be concerns about the potential problems that this could cause. Here the question is the type of business that you might be asked to undertake and the potential for your firm to be caught up in illegal activities. Are you confident that you can identify these and deal with them appropriately, or would the safest course of action be to decline at the outset?

Although the current regime in Suburbia does not have a very savoury reputation, the fact that our government is able to do business with them, notwithstanding that we have granted political asylum to a former citizen, suggests that political pragmatism is overriding any ethical scruples that may be held. You are faced with similar considerations.

The reality is likely to be that whatever dealings Alexander has, directly or indirectly, with Suburbia are unlikely to be in his own name and would be several steps removed from him. Is this likely to be sufficient to protect your firm, even if you make clear that you are prepared to undertake only personal business for Alexander? A problem to which this may lead is that part of the justification for taking on Alexander is that he will introduce further clients to you, but they may be less acceptable than he is, thus putting you in the position of declining to do business with his "friends".

OPTIMUM SOLUTION

At the end of the day the question relates to the Bank's judgment of the risk in taking on Alexander, compared with the potential reward, neither of which is very clear cut. Erring on the side of caution one might say that this is business which you should allow to pass, but the argument for that is no stronger than the argument that taking on Alexander as a client is in the interests of the bank.

Your considerations might, therefore, be divided under For and Against, as follows:

For:

- This potential new client could represent the start of valuable new business, in line with your mandate from the board.
- This client could lead to further profitable business.
- Bruce has previous, satisfactory experience of Alexander while at his former bank.
- There is no record of anything untoward in respect of Alexander during the past five years.
- The prosecution for bribery occurred six years ago and the charges may well have been "trumped up".
- Alexander has been admitted to the UK having successfully sought asylum.
- The rumours and negative comment concerning Alexander are historic and anecdotal.
- There has been recent favourable media comment concerning the financial investment in jobs and infrastructure by Alexander in a disadvantaged part of the UK.

Against:

- You have received a written risk intelligence report raising questions as to the probity of Alexander.
- Alexander might still be prosecuted for any former wrongdoing in Suburbia.
- Alexander might still be operating in an illegal manner in Suburbia.
- Your board have, thus far, displayed a cautious approach to risk and is strongly averse to the possibility of any reputational damage.

POSSIBLE COURSES OF ACTION

In continuing to adopt your bank's traditional risk-averse approach, you must balance the value of new business against the possibility of being caught up in money laundering charges or other problems arising from the history of Alexander. However, your bank's possibly oversensitive attitude has contributed materially to the performance of your bank falling behind that of its peer group.

To avoid any risk of reputational damage, the bank could simply decline to open the account but the new account opening committee should discuss the proposal with an open mind. As chief executive you might consider having a prior discussion with your board in order to review the bank's attitude to risk, balanced against the need to increase profitability.

RECOMMENDATION

As a matter of "realpolitik" acceptance of clients with this type of uncertain history is likely to become more common and, in this instance where the negative features about Alexander are rather sketchy, it would be sensible to give him the benefit of the doubt.

However, in accepting Alexander it should be remembered that the maximum opportunity to control any situation is before a client is taken on board and it is considerably more difficult afterwards. Accordingly, both you and the client should be quite clear on the scope of business which you are likely to be offered and the terms on which you are prepared to accept it, so as to avoid problems at a later date. Equally, it will help management to keep a careful watching brief on the account which, it should be recognised, may require substantial time and resource.

QUICK READ SUMMARY

A MATTER OF REPUTATION

What is/would be unethical

It would be unethical to take Alexander as a customer solely on the basis of the perceived ability of a relationship with him to generate significant amount of income for your bank, together with the prospect of introduction of further clients. You must be aware of Alexander's antecedents and accordingly must make proper enquiry. Similarly, if your enquiries raise some questions, these must be properly considered rather than ignored as being of no consequence.

Key points summary

Your bank is falling behind its rivals in attracting wealthy clients.

You have the opportunity to begin a potentially profitable relationship with a wealthy expatriate, but background checks raise a number of warning flags.

Do you ignore these because of the client's potential value, or should you give these full consideration, the implications notwithstanding?

Adverse consequences

Depending upon your point of view, there are potentially adverse consequences in both directions:

Spending time investigating Alexander's background and then questioning him about anything adverse that your research reveals might cause him to think that he would rather deal with one of your competitors, who may be less scrupulous.

Alternatively, failing to carry out proper background checks, or ignoring what they reveal, might result in your bank becoming involved in a variety of problematical situations to its direct (financial) and indirect (reputational) detriment, but which could easily have been avoided.

Optimum approach

Carry out proper background checks. Be guided by what you find and openly debate the issues. If you then feel comfortable with a relationship, ensure that the parameters are quite clear.

SII Code of Conduct impact

Principle 2 – to act with integrity in fulfilling the responsibilities of your appointment.

Principle 7 – to strive to uphold the highest personal standards, including rejecting short-term profits which may jeopardise your reputation and that of your employer.

CREATIVE ACCOUNTING

Servicing the requirements of a valuable client requires "creative accounting" fully to recover your firm's costs.

BACKGROUND

You are the chief executive of a small, regional finance company which has a good track record of providing financial support to facilitate local infrastructure developments aimed at helping the local community. Before committing financial assistance, your company always researches such developments very thoroughly in order to minimise the risk of default and has developed a good reputation as a responsible lender, and strong supporter of the region in which it operates.

One of your relationship managers brings you a proposal to provide substantial financing for a complex infrastructure development in the heart of the region, which will bring substantial social benefits to the community and welcome revenue to your company, while further enhancing its positive reputation. However, significant prior research will be required before the firm could commit to the financing, given the size and complexity of the proposed development.

Because of the nature of the project, which also involves significant public funding, you have been advised that reimbursement of your research costs may be available from Ruination, a public body which exists to encourage financial investment and support in the region. On enquiring further into the nature of this reimbursement you learn that the daily rate payable is substantially below the economic cost of having members of your team research the viability of the development project.

Ruination will pay a centrally imposed standard rate of £1,000 per day, plus "reasonable expenses" whereas your firm's internal cost of assigning an appropriate team to this exercise would be £2,000 per day. On discussing this matter with your relationship manager he tells you that he has been speaking with a contact at Ruination who has indicated, informally, that it would be quite relaxed if your firm simply charges for a sufficient number of days to cover your costs, effectively inflating the size of the claim. Additionally, this contact has indicated that Ruination's daily reimbursement rate is based upon a five hour working day, compared with your firm's normal requirement for its employees to work a seven hour day. Your manager has been told that reimbursement of claims constructed to take account of differences between Ruination's reimbursement rate and clients' charging rates is accepted practice, and everyone involved is aware of it.

If you adopt this method of claiming reimbursement for time spent on research, you should be able fully to recover the cost of the time which your team will need to spend researching the viability of the proposed project.

THE DILEMMA

The infrastructure project is expected to be of great public benefit and your firm's involvement would give it a high public profile. Consequently, you are keen to assist, subject to the outcome of the viability study which must be completed first. However, because of the size and complexity of the project, you are concerned that it will be necessary to spend more time than usual on research, which will be expensive in terms of man hours that would need to be spent by your team. Accordingly, you are keen to receive full reimbursement for their time, particularly in the event that your firm decides not to grant the financing.

What factors might you consider?

- The basic rate of reimbursement for time spent is not economic.
- A possible alternative method of claiming for time spent has been suggested, albeit in an informal manner.
- This "informal" practice is commonplace and acceptable to Ruination.
- No-one else will know that you would be claiming for a greater number of days than would actually be worked.
- Potentially this could lead to highly remunerative business for your firm.
- This is a very worthwhile project for the local community, with high visibility for those involved.

ISSUES

Your firm enjoys a good reputation, which you wish to retain. You wish to assist with the financing, subject to the viability study. In contemplating making claims for reimbursement based on an inflated number of days, you are concerned that you may risk future reputational damage if it becomes public knowledge.

OPTIMUM SOLUTION

You could simply claim the contractual rate of reimbursement on offer for the actual number of hours worked and have your firm absorb the additional costs involved.

You could adopt the suggested system of reimbursement and invoice Ruination for a sufficient number of days to cover your actual costs, thus ensuring that you received full reimbursement of your normal charging rate.

You could request formal confirmation of the reimbursement method suggested by your Ruination contact.

In considering which course of action is most appropriate, you will have to decide how valuable this potential business may be to your firm. Acceptance of the reduced consultancy fee may be a small price to pay for actually securing the business which would result from being awarded the mandate to provide finance. This would provide comfort that you have not indulged in any activity which might sully the reputation of your firm.

Although Ruination accepts that its reimbursement rates are out of line with the market and thus indulges in "old Spanish customs" to provide reimbursement at market rates, this is not a policy which is likely to gain public endorsement. Consequently, if your part in it comes to light, your firm is likely to receive as much criticism as Ruination.

Accordingly, the best course of action is to try to negotiate an acceptable rate of reimbursement with Ruination. If this is not possible you will have to decide how valuable your firm's total involvement will be if you do become the project financier and perhaps more critically, whether you would still wish to carry out the viability study, bearing in mind that it may reveal that the project is not viable.

Having a clear conscience should be more important than the possibility of having to trim your fees which, in this case, represent your charge out rate, rather than actual cost.

QUICK READ SUMMARY

CREATIVE ACCOUNTING

What is/would be unethical

Strictly speaking it would be unethical to submit an invoice that does not comply with the terms of your contract of engagement. The fact that Ruination is aware of, and condones, this practice only makes the dilemma more acute.

Key points summary

You represent a firm that carries out consultancy work and provides project finance.

You have the opportunity to bid for a consultancy project which could result in a valuable financing opportunity for your firm.

Costs of the initial viability study would be reimbursed at a rate significantly below your firm's usual charge out rate.

The client has an informal understanding with consultants, which enables its invoices to be structured in such a way that it provides full reimbursement, as well as meeting the client's centrally imposed rates of reimbursement.

Adverse consequences

The potential adverse consequences to your firm are principally that of reputational damage, should you submit an invoice in the manner which you have been advised, albeit "informally", is acceptable and are then challenged to demonstrate that it complies with the terms of the contract.

Since obviously it does not, you might then be barred from tendering for further work, not only with Ruination, but also a wider spread of public bodies.

From the perspective of your firm, there is an additional consideration if you honestly believe that the reimbursement rate is uneconomic and that you are not confident that the project is either viable, or that your firm will receive the financing mandate.

Optimum approach

The most appropriate course of action is to seek formal confirmation from Ruination of its rate of reimbursement for time spent, the terms of business that it will and will not accept and then to decide whether you wish still to bid for the contract on that basis.

SII Code of Conduct impact

Principle 1 – to act honestly and fairly at all times when dealing with clients…

Principle 2 – to act with integrity in fulfilling the responsibilities of your appointment.

Principle 7 – to strive to uphold the highest personal standards, including rejecting short-term profits.

WORLD TOUR

A new director visits your overseas operations where his behaviour causes concern about his suitability for a more senior role.

BACKGROUND

You are a senior manager in an international business, where the chairman's scheduled retirement date is approaching. The firm has recently appointed a new non-executive director, Richard, who has been identified as a possible future chairman. As a part of his familiarisation process with the business, Richard has undertaken a series of visits to overseas offices of your firm and on a number of these he was accompanied by members of your team.

These visits involved you in liaising with colleagues overseas, to ensure that Richard was introduced to appropriate representatives of the firm, as well as important local business leaders and government representatives. Consequently, all the visits were high profile and press coverage was encouraged and quite successful.

However, you are concerned at feedback that you have received from members of your team who accompanied Richard on a number of these visits and you wonder quite how you should deal with it.

The reason for this unease relates to two specific incidents involving Richard, one public and one private, which occurred during the trips, stages of which were unavoidably long and tiring, with lengthy travelling days ending in major receptions. During one of these journeys, Richard had liberally enjoyed the refreshments available in the first class section of the aircraft and had been very effusive to the crew on disembarking. This flight was followed by a short break at a hotel, where a large reception had been arranged, at which Richard met senior members of your local staff, local business leaders and a number of government representatives.

Your team member, Stephanie, tells you that during the course of the reception, it appeared to her that Richard was drinking a lot and, on top of the alcohol consumed on the flight, it was impairing his speech. Additionally, he seemed to be concentrating heavily on entertaining the female guests, including Stephanie, who were made to feel very uncomfortable by his close attention. Richard was reluctant to talk to the local dignitaries towards whom Stephanie and the local executives were trying to steer him and made a number of remarks about them which, although possibly jocular, might have caused offence.

A further incident was reported to you by an overseas colleague, Mark, who had attended another reception for Richard at which he had been overly attentive to a female guest who was one of Mark's valued clients, inviting her out to dinner, to which Mark conspicuously was not invited. The client mentioned this subsequently to Mark, saying that she had accepted the dinner invitation only to avoid causing a scene and that she was not at all happy about it, suggesting that she was unsure whether she actually wanted to remain a client of your firm.

THE DILEMMA

These two incidents concern you as they reflect, or have the potential to reflect, badly on the firm and if Richard's behaviour extends towards members of the staff, could easily result in litigation. Accordingly, you feel that they must be reported, although you are not quite sure to whom and this causes you considerable unease. However, after discussion with a colleague, you make an appointment to see the chief executive and tell him what has been reported to you.

Although the chief executive tells you that you have done the right thing in advising him of what happened, at this stage he does not feel inclined to take it any further and you get the impression that he had rather not been told. Satisfied that you have taken appropriate action, you advise Stephanie and Mark that you have reported the incidents to the chief executive and that the matter rests with him.

A month later, following a further overseas trip on which Richard was again accompanied by Stephanie, she returns in an agitated state and tells you that Richard made a number of quite suggestive remarks to her, which had an obvious inference. She is very upset and tells you that unless something is done about it she will feel compelled to speak to a solicitor.

You assure Stephanie that you will see that something is done, but having reported previous incidents to the chief executive and been told to ignore them, privately you wonder what you should do. This is an obviously delicate and possibly career-threatening move if you get it wrong but, by the same token, if you ignore it and matters escalate, the impact on the firm and possibly yourself, might be just as serious. Equally, both the firm and you have a moral and legal responsibility of care towards Stephanie and your clients.

There are a number of options open to you:

- Go back to the chief executive. Arguably this is the most sensible because having reported the original instances to the chief executive, he must now be faced with the further evidence. But what do you do if he tells you again to ignore matters, particularly since his reaction on the first occasion appeared slightly hostile?
- Alternatively, you can report the matter to the HR director as the senior staff member for personnel issues. You will need to ensure that he is fully aware of your previous discussion with the chief executive. The problem with this is that the HR director may go only as far as the chief executive, leading to the same lack of action as above.
- You might report your concerns to the senior independent director, again advising him of your previous report to the chief executive, but this might be regarded as a high risk strategy, escalating the matter to this extent.

Given the manner in which this situation has developed, to the point at which litigation resulting from Richard's behaviour is quite possible, your correct course of action is to report the latest incident to the HR director. However, it would be appropriate to advise the chief executive in the first instance, saying that there has been a further incident. You should add that you will have to report to the HR director, as it follows a formal complaint to you and that if you don't report the incident, Stephanie certainly will.

That should be sufficient to persuade the chief executive to take the matter seriously.

QUICK READ SUMMARY

WORLD TOUR

What is/would be unethical

As you have been specifically told about an incident of inappropriate behaviour it would be unethical to try to "sweep it under the carpet", and then to persuade your young colleague not to make a fuss, because of the seniority of the other person involved.

Key points summary

Your firm has recently appointed a new non-executive director, Richard, and sent him to visit some of your overseas offices. A report is made to you by your assistant about Richard's inappropriate behaviour. You receive a further report from another member of staff about Richard's behaviour towards a key client. This requires delicate handling and you report the matter to the chief executive. A further incident is reported to you by a member of staff, who was the subject of unwelcome advances from Richard and who will instruct solicitors unless some positive action is taken.

Adverse consequences

Failure to take action could be damaging on two fronts. If your colleague takes legal action against your firm it is the type of case which might well receive unwelcome publicity, given the parties involved. Additionally, there appears to be a considerable risk of Richard repeating his unacceptable behaviour towards clients and other influential figures which could be directly damaging to the business.

Optimum approach

Discuss the matter fully with the HR director, making it clear that you reported the earlier incidents to the chief executive and that you have also let him know about this latest incident, which has given rise to a formal complaint.

Accordingly, the firm will have to take positive action as the problem will not go away.

It is important that the firm makes quite clear that a culture of inappropriate behaviour will not be tolerated.

SII Code of Conduct impact

Principle 2 – to act with integrity...seek to avoid any acts...which damage the reputation of your organisation...which are improper ... to promote high standards of conduct throughout your organisation.

Principle 7 – to strive to uphold the highest personal standards.

DOES DOING BUSINESS ETHICALLY AFFECT CORPORATE PERFORMANCE?

By Simon Webley, Research Director of the Institute of Business Ethics

Whatever diagnosis one chooses to explain the causes of the world financial malaise in the winter of 2008/09, if it does not include the failure of many financial sector leaders to adhere to basic ethical principles, it is likely to be incomplete.

One commentator has put it this way: "What began as a financial recession has become an ethics recession". In a letter to the Prime Minister in April 2009, the Pope said that "a key element of the crisis is a deficit of ethics in economic structures". The lack of integrity and prudence (when using money belonging to someone else), has caused a major breakdown of trust between financial institutions, businesses and even individuals.

Whose numbers do you believe? Whose predictions do you trust? No-one seems to be sure.

This lack of trust between finance professionals and other institutions is new, though not unprecedented. What flows from it is a deeply-felt anxiety throughout the commercial and political worlds about the stability and sustainability of the national, and even world, financial system. Its impact on corporate performance is also serious. Among other things, it has done nothing to redress the low public esteem in which leaders of business are held.

Opinion polls in Great Britain over recent decades indicate that business leaders, including those of the banks, remain stubbornly in the bottom third of those trusted to tell the truth, along with politicians and journalists. (Doctors are the most trusted – see Chart 1 overleaf).

Chart 1: Public Perception: Trust in integrity of business

Q) Who would you generally trust to tell the truth or not?

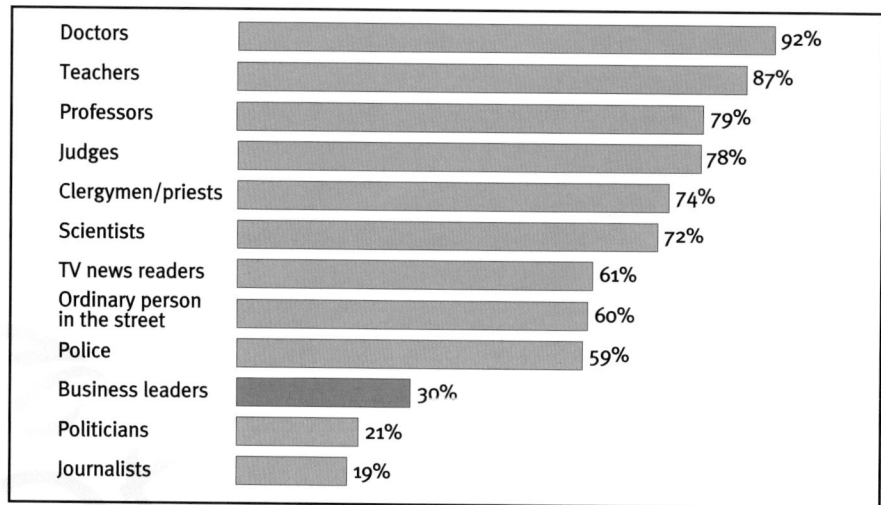

Doctors	92%
Teachers	87%
Professors	79%
Judges	78%
Clergymen/priests	74%
Scientists	72%
TV news readers	61%
Ordinary person in the street	60%
Police	59%
Business leaders	30%
Politicians	21%
Journalists	19%

Base: 2,029 British adults aged 16+, November 2008. Source: Ipsos Mori/RCP.

International data on levels of public trust in business shows that the problem is not confined to the UK (see Chart 2). Only in eight of the 21 countries in the survey do more than half the respondents trust business.

Chart 2: International trust in business

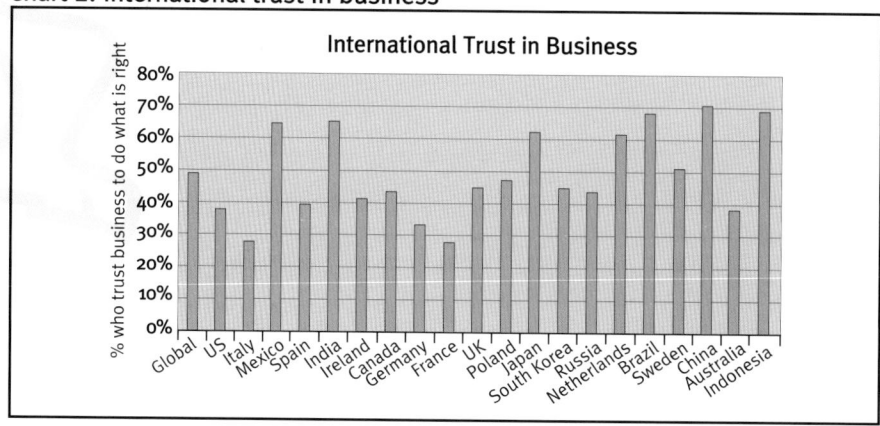

International Trust in Business

Source: Adapted from Edelman Trust Barometer, 2009[1].

[1] Edelman Trust Barometer – 10th edition, 4,475 people in 20 countries in five continents, aged 25-64, college educated, in top 25 per cent of household income per age group in each country.

Mistrust of Business

What is the basis for distrust of business leaders? One explanation is that greed, rather than service, is too often attributed as the sole motive for doing business. The public has voiced its concern through the media about rewards for apparent failure and the size of the annual bonuses particularly in the financial sector.

A series of well-publicised business scandals in the 1990s, (for instance in the UK, the Barings Bank fraud and Robert Maxwell's plundering of the Mirror Group's pension fund), was followed in the US by some high profile incidents in the 2000s. Examples include dishonest and illegal behaviour by senior executives in Enron, WorldCom and Arthur Andersen. In continental Europe, Parmalat and Siemens have both been the victims of conspicuous examples of unethical and illegal behaviour, mainly by senior executives. In India, Satyam Computer Services, with its senior officers' blatant false accounting, shows that emerging economies are not exempt from such problems. These and other ethical lapses reinforce public suspicion of business behaviour and basic honesty.

But it is not only the big organisations that misbehave; local news media is constantly reporting illegal and unethical practice by smaller organisations. These range from poor treatment of employees, customers being "taken for a ride" and the serious results of some larger businesses not paying their invoices according to contract.

Can business leaders restore public trust?

One reason for the poor regard that people have for business people and their integrity is that their leaders rarely discuss business values and ethics in public or even in private. As a result, there tends to be reluctance among employees, as well as some independent directors, to question decisions of management or raise concerns, especially in difficult economic conditions, for fear of unpopularity or even reprisal.

The reticence of leaders to speak up about standards in commercial life may be due first, to a disinclination to "stick their head above the parapet"; and second, because of uncertainty about the business case for insisting on high ethical standards in "the way we do business". If a link could be established between always doing business responsibly and consistently good financial performance, then there would be more reason for directors of companies to speak up about, and insist on, high ethical standards in their organisations. This includes policy and strategy decisions in the boardroom, integrity throughout their organisations and in their relations with all those with whom they do business. As explained later, it is feasible to make such a link.

The Response

Research[2] shows more business leaders now understand that "the way they do business" is an important aspect of fulfilling their financial obligations to their stockholders, as well as other stakeholders. They are responding to accusations of poor behavioural standards in different ways. For instance, more companies are putting in place corporate responsibility policies or ethics policies. The principal feature of these is a code of ethics/conduct/behaviour to guide their staff.

Some economic sectors ie, defence and chemicals have drawn up sector-wide standards. Larger companies now accept that an ethics policy is one of the essential ingredients of good corporate governance.

Modern corporate governance procedures include risk assessments. Until recently these tended to be confined to financial, legal and safety hazards of the organisation. But growing numbers are recognising reputation issues around lack of integrity as a possible source of future problems. Royal Dutch Shell identifies this among its Risk Factors in its 2008 Annual Review:

"An erosion of Shell's business reputation would adversely impact our licence to operate, our brand, our ability to secure new resources and our financial performance."

---

[2] Webley S. & Werner A., Employee Views of Ethics at Work, Institute of Business Ethics, 2009.

Business Values

At the heart of these types of response is board insistence that the organisation will do its business on the basis of agreed and explicit core values. These normally consist of business values (profitability, efficiency) and ethical values (honesty, integrity, fairness etc). According to the Cadbury Report in 1992[3], employees at all levels of an organisation are entitled to guidance on how to resolve ethical dilemmas that they may encounter in the course of their day-to-day business life. But can the time and effort put into designing and implementing such guidance, including a code of conduct/ethics/practice, be shown to make a difference? In other words, does doing business ethically pay?

Research

Recent studies have provided a positive answer to this question. In 2002/03 the Institute of Business Ethics (IBE) undertook research showing that, for large UK companies, having an ethics policy (a code) operating for at least five years, correlated with above average financial performance based on four measures of value. The performance of a control cohort of similar companies without an explicit ethics policy – no code – was used for comparison. This was published by IBE in April 2003 under the title 'Does Business Ethics Pay?'[4]

The methodology developed for this project was used in a more recent study by researchers at Cranfield University and the IBE using more up-to-date data. They came to a similar conclusion.[5]

So what makes the difference? A pilot study described in an Appendix to this report investigated the distinguishing features, if any, of the operations of companies with explicit ethics policies compared with those with a less robust policy.

The business case for paying attention to ethics, while a second order question, can be argued by using some non- financial indicators.

3 Report of the Committee on the Financial Aspects of Corporate Governance, 1992.

4 Webley, S. & More, E. Does Business Ethics Pay? Ethics and financial performance. Institute of Business Ethics, 2003.

5 Ugoji, K., Dando, N. & Moir, L. Does Business Ethics Pay? Revisited: The value of ethics training. Institute of Business Ethics, 2007.

The Reputation Institute in the US uses a reputation quotient to measure companies based on its findings that people regularly justify their feelings about companies on 20 attributes. These they group into six conceptual categories: Emotional appeal, Vision & leadership, Products & services, Workplace environment, Social responsibility, and Financial performance. Work of this sort helps to clarify the use of opinion-based approaches to assess the impact of ethics policies and programmes.

Employee Retention

One non-financial indicator is the retention of high quality staff. This is recognised as important to a profitable and sustainable organisation. The Industrial Society's (now known as The Work Foundation) survey of 255 UK professionals in 2000 indicates that there is increasing pressure on companies to become "employers of choice" as a way to recruit and retain best talent.[6] 82 per cent of people surveyed said they would not work for an organisation whose values they did not believe in. Some 59 per cent said that they chose the company they work for because they believe in what it does and what it stands for. Further, 85 per cent of UK workers agree that knowing that the company they work for is engaged in activities that help to improve society would /does increase their loyalty to their company.

The attraction and retention of high quality staff would be expected to be reflected in higher productivity and ultimately, profitability. This is well explained in *'Putting the Service-Profit Chain to Work'* [7] in which the authors describe the links in the service-profit chain. They argue that profit and growth are stimulated by customer loyalty; loyalty is a direct result of customer satisfaction; satisfaction is largely influenced by the value of services provided to customers; value is created by satisfied, loyal and productive employees; and employee satisfaction, in turn, results from high quality support services and policies that enable employees to deliver results to customers.

[6] Draper.S. Corporate Nivernah, Industrial Society (renamed Work Foundation), London, 2000.

[7] James L. Heskett, Thomas O. Jones, Gary W. Loveman, W. Earl, Jr. Sasser, Leonard A. Schlesinger Putting the Profit Chain to Work, HBR, July/August 2008.

Customer Retention

A second non-financial indicator is customer retention; it too, is recognised as a significant factor in the long term viability of a company. A research paper in 2002[8] showed that corporate ethical character makes a difference in the way that customers (and other stakeholders) identify with the company (brand awareness). The author argues that this connection is an "emotional one" when it comes to stakeholders and is not all about business measurables.

Besides maintaining good staff and customers, how providers of finance and insurance rate an organisation is a major factor in determining the cost of each. What ratings agencies have developed, with varying degrees of success, are measures of risk – the lower the risk, the lower the capital cost. One study, using Standard and Poor's and Barclays Bank data, has indicated that companies with an explicit ethics policy generally have a higher rating than those without one. This in turn generated a significantly lower cost of capital.[9]

These approaches to assessing the business case for adopting explicit policies and programmes are summarised overleaf:

[8] Chun. R An Alternative Approach to Appraising Corporate Social Performance: Stakeholder Emotion. Manchester Business School. Submitted to Academy of Management Conference, Denver, Colorado, 2002.

[9] Webley. S and Hamilton. K: How Does Business Ethics Pay? In Appendix 3: Does Business Ethics Pay? Revisited, 2007, op.cit.

Summary of the Relations of Ethics Policy to Financial Performance

Corporate Ethical Structure
- Board Policy
- Resources and implementation plan
- Training
- Progress measurement
- Performance evaluation
- Periodic review and reporting

Ethical 'Signalling'
- Managed:
- codes of conduct
- reporting and advice provision
- Unmanaged:
- regulatory compliance reports
- media coverage

Influence on Stakeholders

Employees
- Enticing top recruits to apply for positions
- Greater loyalty
- Motivating factor for employees
- Good working practices resulting in employee satisfaction

Customers
- Greater loyalty
- Increased brand reputation
- Less risk of consumer boycotts
- Emotional factors: association with trust, integrity, satisfaction and distinctiveness.
- Product safety and quality

Investors/Shareholders
- Perceived reduction in 'riskiness' of company as applied values and ethics is an indication of:
- management quality
- ability to handle shocks
- management of stakeholders
- good governance
- competitive advantage

Financial Impacts
- Recruitment of better staff leading to competitive advantage
- Lower costs associated with decrease in employee turnover
- Higher employee productivity
- Lower costs associated with employee disputes

Financial Impacts
- Premium prices for products
- More stable or greater revenues
- Intangible and brand value increases

Financial Impacts
- Cheaper cost of equity capital
- Market value of equity increased
- Credit risk reduced and consequently cost of borrowing falls
- Insurance premiums reduced

What is apparent from these research projects, and others in the US, is that the leadership of consistently well-managed companies accepts that having a corporate responsibility/ethics policy is an important part of their corporate governance agenda. It is also noteworthy that companies with ethics policies and codes are consistently recorded as more admired by their peer group compared with those which are not explicit about ethics.[10] In other words, maintaining a high standard of ethical behaviour is seen by them to be a critical element of a company's culture and reputation.

It can, of course, be argued that leaders of businesses which pay more than lip service to maintaining ethical standards do not need any assurance that their approach to the way they do business will also enhance their profitability: they know it to be true. Indeed, having an ethics policy can be said to be one hallmark of a well-managed organisation. But others need convincing.

The aftermath of the turmoil in the financial sector in the winter of 2008/09 provides the opportunity to reassess these matters.

[10] Op.cit. Footnote 2.